The Paperclip Collector

Small Things Matter

Keith Reed

Chapter 1: The Art of Collecting

The Psychology Behind Collecting

Collecting is a deeply ingrained aspect of human nature, stemming from our innate desire to find order and meaning in a chaotic world. It transcends simple hoarding; it is a purposeful pursuit that taps into psychological, emotional, and even social dimensions of our lives. Understanding the psychology behind collecting reveals why individuals find joy and fulfillment in amassing seemingly trivial items, like paperclips, and how these objects can come to symbolize much more than their practical uses.

At the core of collecting lies a fundamental need for control. In an unpredictable world, the act of gathering and organizing objects provides a sense of stability. For many collectors, each item represents a piece of a larger puzzle, a tangible manifestation of their interests and passions. The meticulous arrangement of a collection can evoke feelings of accomplishment and satisfaction, creating a sanctuary where the collector feels empowered. This need for control can manifest in various forms, from the way items are displayed to the very nature of the items chosen for the collection. For instance, a paperclip collector might delight in organizing their collection by color, size, or even historical significance, finding comfort in the systematic nature of it all.

Moreover, collecting often serves as a narrative tool, allowing individuals to weave personal stories into the fabric of their lives. Each piece in a collection can evoke memories or emotions tied to specific experiences. A collector might remember the day they found a unique paperclip at a flea market, or the joy of receiving a rare item as a gift. These memories imbue the objects with significance, transforming them from mere items into cherished artifacts of one's life journey. This emotional connection is a powerful motivator for collectors, as it fosters a sense of attachment and belonging.

The act of collecting also plays a crucial role in identity formation. Individuals often collect items that reflect their personal values, beliefs, or interests, allowing them to communicate aspects of their identity to the world. A collector who focuses on paperclips may be drawn to the creativity and innovation behind their designs, or perhaps the simplicity and utility they represent. This choice can signal a desire to embrace minimalism or to celebrate everyday objects that often go unnoticed. In this way, collecting becomes a form of self-expression, enabling individuals to curate a narrative about who they are and what they value.

Social interaction is another pivotal element in the psychology of collecting. Communities of collectors often form around shared interests, providing a sense of belonging and camaraderie. Online forums, social media groups, and local meet-ups foster connections among individuals who might otherwise feel isolated in their pursuits. These interactions can create a rich tapestry of shared knowledge and experiences, where collectors exchange stories about rare finds, trade items, or even collaborate on projects. The relationships built within these communities can be deeply rewarding, reinforcing the idea that collecting is not just a solitary endeavor but a shared journey.

Competition can also fuel the passion for collecting. The thrill of the hunt—the pursuit of rare or unique items—can be exhilarating. The desire to possess something that others do not can create a sense of urgency and excitement. For some, the challenge lies in finding items that are not only rare but also have an interesting history or story behind them. This competitive spirit can drive collectors to explore new places, attend shows, and engage with different communities, enriching their collecting experience even further.

However, the psychological aspects of collecting are not without their darker sides. For some individuals, the urge to collect can become obsessive, leading to hoarding behaviors that can disrupt their lives. When the pursuit of collecting overshadows other responsibilities or relationships, it can result in a negative impact on mental health. Recognizing the fine line between healthy collecting and compulsive behavior is essential. A successful collector often maintains balance, ensuring that their passion does not detract from their overall well-being.

The psychology of collecting also taps into the concept of nostalgia. Many collectors are drawn to items that evoke memories of their past, allowing them to reconnect with simpler times or cherished moments. A paperclip from a childhood art project or a unique design that recalls a favorite teacher can evoke powerful emotions. This connection to the past can be comforting, providing a sense of continuity in an ever-changing world. Collecting transforms these small objects into vessels of nostalgia, allowing individuals to hold onto memories that might otherwise fade.

As we delve into the complexities of collecting, it becomes evident that the motivations are layered and multifaceted. From the desire for control and identity to the thrill of social interaction and nostalgia, the reasons individuals collect are as diverse as the items they gather. Each collector's journey is unique, shaped by personal experiences, cultural influences, and individual psychology.

In this intricate dance of emotions and motivations, it is the small things—like a simple paperclip—that can hold profound significance. The act of collecting is not merely about the accumulation of objects; it is a reflection of who we are, how we navigate our world, and the connections we forge along the way. Embracing this understanding can enhance the joy of collecting, transforming it into a lifelong journey rich with meaning and personal significance.

Types of Collectors

Collecting is a diverse and colorful tapestry woven from the passions and interests of individuals from all walks of life. Each collector is distinct, driven by their own motivations, preferences, and stories. Understanding the various types of collectors illuminates the rich landscape of this hobby and reveals the unique ways people find joy in gathering objects.

Some collectors are driven by the thrill of the hunt. They thrive on the excitement of discovering rare items, whether in antique shops, estate sales, or flea markets. These avid treasure seekers often possess a keen eye for detail and an intuitive sense for spotting potential gems hidden among the mundane. The adrenaline rush of finding a long-sought-after piece can be intoxicating, and for many, the chase is as rewarding as the acquisition itself. This type of collector enjoys the journey, often developing deep knowledge about their area of interest. They might spend hours researching the history of a specific item, learning about its makers, and connecting with other enthusiasts who share their passion.

On the other end of the spectrum lies the completionist. For these collectors, the goal is often to gather every item within a particular category or series. This quest for completeness can be all-consuming, pushing them to acquire not only the most coveted pieces but also the less glamorous ones that fill gaps in their collections. Take, for instance, someone collecting paperclips. They might seek out every variation from classic metal designs to quirky shapes and colors. Completionists can find satisfaction in the meticulous organization of their collections, often displaying them in a way that showcases the full spectrum of their hard work. The sense of accomplishment felt upon adding the final item to a collection can be immensely gratifying, providing a sense of closure and fulfillment.

Conversely, some collectors are drawn to the aesthetic appeal of the items themselves. For them, the beauty and design of an object are paramount. This type of collector may find joy in curating a collection of visually striking paperclips, perhaps focusing on those with unique shapes, colors, or artistic designs. They might enjoy arranging their items in a way that showcases their creativity, often using displays to tell a visual story. These collectors often view their items as art, appreciating not just the function they serve but the artistry behind their creation. This perspective can inspire them to explore a wide array of designs, leading to a collection that celebrates beauty in all its forms.

Nostalgia plays a powerful role for many collectors, particularly those who seek items that connect them to their past. These collectors are often motivated by memories, searching for objects that evoke a sense of longing for times gone by. A collector might be drawn to vintage paperclips that remind them of their school days, recalling the simple pleasure of using them to hold together important papers. Each item becomes a vessel for memories, and the act of collecting transforms into a journey of self-reflection and sentimentality. For these individuals, the emotional connection to their items enriches the experience, making each find a personal treasure that tells a story.

There are also collectors who focus on the historical context of their items. These individuals are often passionate about preserving pieces of the past, whether it be through collecting artifacts, memorabilia, or even everyday objects like paperclips. They may research the cultural significance of their collections, exploring how these items reflect societal changes over time. A paperclip collector, for example, might delve into the evolution of the paperclip design, examining its use during different historical periods and its role in the workplace. This type of collector often sees themselves as a steward of history, dedicated to keeping the stories of the past alive through their collections.

Then, there are the socially motivated collectors who find community and connection through their shared interests. These individuals are often active participants in collecting clubs or online forums, engaging in discussions and exchanges with fellow enthusiasts. They might organize events, exhibitions, or swap meets, fostering a sense of camaraderie among like-minded individuals. For them, the experience of collecting is as much about the relationships built along the way as it is about the items themselves. Whether trading paperclips or sharing stories behind their collections, these collectors thrive on the connections they forge with others who understand their passion.

Some collectors embrace a more eclectic approach, driven by a love for variety and the unexpected. These collectors may not limit themselves to one specific category or theme; instead, they gather a broad array of items that catch their interest. A collector might have a fascination with both vintage paperclips and quirky kitchen gadgets, enjoying the diversity of their collection. This type of collector often revels in the unpredictability of their finds, cherishing the serendipity of discovering unexpected treasures that add depth and character to their gatherings.

The motivations and styles of collectors are as varied as the items they seek. Each type of collector brings a unique perspective to the hobby, contributing to a vibrant community rich with shared stories and experiences. Understanding these different types enhances appreciation for the act of collecting itself, revealing the many ways individuals express their passions and connect with the world around them. Whether driven by nostalgia, aesthetics, social connections, or the thrill of the hunt, collectors unite in their love for the small, often overlooked items that hold profound significance in their lives. Ultimately, the act of collecting becomes a celebration of individuality, creativity, and the intricate tapestry of human experience.

The Evolution of Collecting

Collecting has been a fundamental aspect of human behavior for centuries, evolving alongside cultural shifts, technological advancements, and societal changes. From the simple gathering of stones and shells in ancient times to the complex, specialized collections of today, the practice of collecting reflects our innate curiosity and desire to preserve history. Understanding how collecting has evolved provides insight into not only the objects we choose to gather but also the motivations and contexts that drive these pursuits.

In ancient civilizations, collecting was often tied to survival and utility. Early humans gathered resources essential for their daily lives, including food, tools, and materials for shelter. As societies developed, so too did the concept of collecting. Wealthy elites began amassing items that demonstrated power and status.

In ancient Rome, for example, the wealthy would collect art, rare artifacts, and exotic items from their conquests. These collections served not only as symbols of wealth but also as a way to connect with the broader world, showcasing the owner's influence and reach.

The Renaissance marked a significant turning point in the history of collecting. During this period, the focus shifted from mere possession to the appreciation of art and culture. Individuals began to collect paintings, sculptures, and manuscripts, driven by a desire to foster knowledge and beauty. This era saw the emergence of cabinets of curiosities—private collections filled with natural wonders, art, and scientific specimens. These cabinets served as a reflection of the collector's identity, and they often became a source of fascination for society at large. The act of collecting transformed into a scholarly pursuit, one that allowed individuals to engage with the world's wonders and mysteries.

As we moved into the 18th and 19th centuries, collecting became more democratized. The Industrial Revolution brought about mass production, making certain items more accessible to the general public. People began to collect everyday objects, such as stamps, coins, and postcards. The establishment of museums further fueled this evolution, as they provided spaces for the public to view and appreciate collections that were once reserved for the elite. The hobby of collecting became a pastime for many, bridging social classes and inviting a broader range of individuals to participate in this enriching pursuit.

The 20th century witnessed yet another transformation in the world of collecting, driven by globalization and technological advancements. The rise of the internet revolutionized how collectors connected with one another. Online marketplaces emerged, enabling individuals to buy, sell, and trade items across the globe. This newfound accessibility allowed collectors to discover unique pieces from different cultures and regions, broadening the scope of what could be collected. No longer confined to local flea markets or antique shops, collectors could now access a world of possibilities at their fingertips.

Additionally, the advent of social media changed the way collectors interacted and shared their passions. Platforms like Instagram and Pinterest became vital spaces for showcasing collections, connecting with fellow enthusiasts, and gaining inspiration. Collectors could now curate their online presence, sharing stories about their favorite items and engaging with a community that transcends geographic boundaries. This shift fostered a sense of belonging and camaraderie, as collectors found support and encouragement from like-minded individuals.

As collecting evolved, so did the types of items that people sought to gather. While traditional collectibles such as stamps, coins, and antiques remained popular, new categories emerged. Pop culture artifacts, such as comic books, action figures, and vintage video games, captured the imaginations of a younger generation. The rise of nostalgia-driven collecting brought forth an appreciation for items that resonate with personal memories, often reflecting the cultural zeitgeist of specific eras. For many, collecting became a way to reconnect with their childhood or to preserve a piece of their history.

Today, sustainability is becoming an increasingly important aspect of collecting. As awareness of environmental issues grows, many collectors are seeking out items that reflect a commitment to eco-friendliness. This includes a focus on vintage and second-hand goods, as well as a preference for items made from sustainable materials. Collectors are now more conscientious about the stories behind their objects, preferring to support artisans and small businesses that align with their values. This evolution in mindset highlights a shift toward responsible collecting, where the emphasis is not just on ownership but on the impact of those choices.

The evolution of collecting is a fascinating journey through time, reflecting broader societal trends and individual passions. From ancient survival instincts to modern expressions of identity and sustainability, the act of collecting reveals much about who we are as a species. Today's collectors are part of a rich tapestry of history, contributing to a legacy that intertwines personal stories, cultural significance, and the preservation of the past. As we continue to navigate an ever-changing world, the practice of collecting will undoubtedly evolve further, adapting to new challenges and opportunities while remaining a cherished form of self-expression and connection. Each item held tightly in our hands carries a narrative, a piece of the story that links us to those who came before us and those who will follow. In this way, collecting remains not just a pastime but a vital expression of the human experience, continuously reshaped by the passage of time and the pulse of our collective lives.

Starting Your Own Collection

Embarking on the journey of collecting can be both thrilling and fulfilling, offering an opportunity to explore personal interests while creating a tangible connection to the world around you. Whether you are drawn to vintage toys, rare stamps, or, perhaps, the humble yet fascinating paperclip, starting your own collection is an adventure that invites curiosity and creativity. The process of building a collection is as much about the items themselves as it is about the experiences and stories that unfold along the way.

Before diving into the world of collecting, it's essential to reflect on what truly captivates you. Consider your interests, hobbies, and passions. Are there specific themes or subjects that resonate with you? Perhaps you have a love for nature, art, history, or technology. Identifying what excites you will serve as the foundation for your collection. This personal connection will not only make the collecting process more enjoyable but will also foster a deeper appreciation for the items you choose to gather.

Once you have a focus, the next step is to research your chosen area. Knowledge is a collector's best friend. Understanding the history, significance, and variations of your chosen items will enrich your experience and empower you to make informed decisions. For instance, if you decide to collect paperclips, you might explore their evolution over time, the different designs available, and the stories behind their creation. This background knowledge will not only enhance your appreciation of your collection but will also serve as a conversation starter with fellow enthusiasts you may encounter.

After gaining a foundational understanding of your area of interest, consider setting specific goals for your collection. Do you want to aim for a certain number of items, or perhaps focus on acquiring specific types or styles? Setting goals can provide direction and motivation as you embark on your collecting journey. However, it's important to remain flexible; collecting is often about the unexpected finds and serendipitous discoveries that can arise along the way. Embrace the journey, allowing your collection to evolve naturally as you uncover new treasures.

With a focus and goals in place, it's time to begin the hunt. This part of the process can be exhilarating, as you explore various sources for acquiring items. Local flea markets, antique shops, thrift stores, and online marketplaces are excellent places to start. Each location offers its own unique charm and potential finds. Engaging in the thrill of the hunt can lead to delightful surprises—perhaps you stumble upon a rare paperclip design or an unexpected piece that complements your collection perfectly.

Networking with other collectors can also yield valuable insights and opportunities. Joining local clubs or online communities can introduce you to fellow enthusiasts who share your passion. These connections can provide tips on where to find items, advice on how to care for your collection, and even opportunities for trading. Additionally, interacting with others in the collecting community can deepen your understanding of your chosen area and inspire new avenues for exploration.

As your collection begins to take shape, consider how you want to display and organize your items. The way you present your collection can enhance its visibility and significance. Whether you choose to display items on shelves, in shadow boxes, or through creative arrangements, think about how each piece tells a story. A carefully curated display can transform your collection into a work of art, inviting admiration and sparking conversations. This aspect of collecting allows you to express your personality and creativity, making your collection truly your own.

Caring for your collection is another vital aspect of the journey. Proper maintenance ensures that your items remain in good condition and can continue to bring you joy for years to come. Research the best practices for preserving the types of items you collect. For example, if you are gathering paperclips, consider storing them in a way that prevents rusting or damage. Understanding how to care for your collection reflects your commitment and passion for the pursuit, adding another layer of meaning to your efforts.

As you gather and nurture your collection, take time to reflect on the stories and memories associated with each item. Every piece holds a narrative—whether it's the thrill of the find, the person who gifted it to you, or the moment you realized its significance. Documenting these stories can add depth to your collection, transforming it into a curated timeline of your interests and experiences. Consider keeping a journal or creating digital records that capture the journey of your collecting adventures.

Finally, remember that collecting is a personal journey, and there is no right or wrong way to go about it. Your collection will evolve based on your interests, experiences, and discoveries. Embrace the process with an open heart and mind, allowing yourself to enjoy the twists and turns along the way. Each item you gather contributes to a larger narrative—one that reflects your unique perspective and passions.

Starting your own collection is an invitation to engage with the world around you in a meaningful way. It encourages exploration, connection, and creativity, all while providing a platform for self-expression. As you embark on this journey, you may discover not only the joy of collecting but also a deeper understanding of yourself and the stories that shape your life. Whether you find solace in the meticulous arrangement of your items or thrill in the hunt for the next great find, the act of collecting becomes a celebration of your individual journey through the vast and vibrant tapestry of human experience.

Chapter 2: The Significance of Small Things

Finding Beauty in the Mundane

Amid the chaos of daily life, there exists a profound beauty in the mundane—those ordinary objects and experiences that often go unnoticed yet hold immense significance. This beauty can be found in the simplest of items, like a paperclip, a coffee cup, or a well-worn book. Embracing the ordinary allows us to cultivate mindfulness and appreciation for the world around us, transforming the everyday into something remarkable.

The journey begins with a shift in perspective. To truly see the beauty in the mundane, one must be willing to slow down and observe the details that typically escape our notice. Consider the paperclip: a small, unassuming object made of metal, designed to hold papers together. At first glance, it may seem trivial, but upon closer inspection, the paperclip's design is a testament to human ingenuity. Its simplicity belies its functionality; it embodies the intersection of form and purpose. Each curve and twist tells a story of practicality, reminding us that even the most ordinary objects can have a significant impact on our lives.

Mindfulness plays a crucial role in this exploration. By practicing mindfulness, we can train ourselves to appreciate the present moment and the objects within it. Take a moment to hold a paperclip in your hand. Feel its cool, smooth surface. Notice the way it bends and flexes with gentle pressure. Contemplate its journey from a factory to your desk. This simple exercise opens a door to deeper awareness, allowing us to find beauty in the everyday.

Engaging with the mundane can also serve as a catalyst for creativity. Artists, writers, and creators often draw inspiration from the ordinary. Think of a painter who captures the play of light on a glass of water, or a poet who finds rhythm in the sound of rain tapping against a window. By focusing on the seemingly insignificant, they elevate the ordinary to extraordinary heights. This act of transformation invites us to reimagine our surroundings, finding new ways to express our thoughts and emotions.

Moreover, finding beauty in the mundane fosters a sense of gratitude. When we acknowledge the small things—a warm cup of coffee, the laughter of a child, or the rustling of leaves in the wind—we cultivate a mindset that values simplicity. This shift can enhance our overall well-being, as studies suggest that practicing gratitude is linked to improved mental health and increased happiness. By recognizing and appreciating the ordinary, we begin to realize that beauty does not always manifest in grand gestures or spectacular events, but rather in the quiet moments of everyday life.

An essential aspect of this journey is the connection to our memories and experiences. The mundane often holds sentimental value, serving as a bridge to our past. A faded photograph, a handwritten letter, or a cherished trinket can evoke powerful emotions and memories. These objects remind us of moments spent with loved ones, milestones achieved, or lessons learned. The beauty of these items lies not only in their physical presence but in the stories they carry. By allowing ourselves to reminisce, we can find profound meaning in the ordinary.

Consider a well-worn book that has been read and reread over the years. Its pages may be dog-eared, and its spine may be creased, yet it holds the wisdom and experiences of countless readers. Each mark tells a story of discovery, of knowledge gained, or of comfort found in its pages. This book is more than just a collection of words; it's a vessel of memories and emotions, a testament to the power of literature to shape our lives. Finding beauty in such an object invites us to reflect on our own journeys and the narratives that define us.

Additionally, the act of collecting ordinary items can become a fulfilling pursuit. By intentionally gathering objects that resonate with us—be it vintage kitchen utensils, quirky mugs, or unique paperclips—we create a personal narrative that reflects our tastes, interests, and values. Each piece in our collection serves as a reminder of our journey, a snapshot of our experiences. This process can be incredibly rewarding, as it encourages us to seek out beauty in the simplest of things and to appreciate their significance.

The beauty in the mundane is also a reminder of our shared humanity. In a world that often glorifies the extraordinary, it is essential to recognize that we all experience the ordinary. The daily rituals of cooking, cleaning, commuting, and working connect us, illustrating the common threads of life. By embracing these experiences, we can foster a sense of empathy and understanding, recognizing that beauty exists in our shared struggles and triumphs.

Finding beauty in the mundane encourages a deeper connection with the world. It invites us to engage with our surroundings and appreciate the small details that contribute to the larger tapestry of life. This perspective shift can lead to a richer, more fulfilling existence, as we learn to celebrate the ordinary moments that often go unnoticed. By cultivating mindfulness, gratitude, and creativity, we can transform our experiences, allowing the mundane to become a source of inspiration and joy.

As we embark on this journey, let us remember that beauty is not confined to the extraordinary; it thrives in the ordinary. By opening our eyes to the world around us, we can discover the elegance in simplicity, the magic in the everyday, and the stories that lie within even the smallest objects. In doing so, we enrich our lives and find connection, purpose, and beauty in every moment.

The Power of Miniature Objects

Miniature objects hold a unique charm that transcends their small size. They invite curiosity, evoke nostalgia, and spark creativity, often serving as powerful symbols of larger concepts and emotions. These little treasures captivate our imagination and remind us that size does not determine significance. From dollhouses filled with tiny furniture to intricate model trains that recreate entire landscapes, miniature objects transport us into worlds that are rich with detail and possibility.

The allure of miniatures can be traced back through history. Ancient civilizations created small-scale replicas of everyday objects, religious artifacts, and even architectural marvels. In ancient Egypt, for instance, artisans crafted miniature offerings for the afterlife, designed to accompany the deceased into the next world. These small items were imbued with great meaning, serving as symbols of sustenance and comfort in the afterlife. Similarly, in Japan, the art of making netsuke—tiny sculptures that served as toggles for traditional clothing—demonstrates the cultural significance of miniature craftsmanship.

As we delve deeper into the world of miniatures, we discover their role in storytelling. Miniature objects often serve as tools for narrative exploration, allowing us to tell complex stories in a compact format. Consider the tradition of dioramas, where scenes are meticulously crafted to depict historical events, natural environments, or fictional tales. These three-dimensional representations invite viewers to step into another world, encouraging them to engage with the story on a personal level. The detail in a diorama can evoke emotions, provoke thoughts, and inspire wonder, all while remaining contained within a small space.

In contemporary art, miniatures continue to play a significant role. Artists use small-scale works to challenge perceptions of value, space, and meaning. The renowned artist Claes Oldenburg, for example, is famous for his whimsical, oversized sculptures of everyday objects. Yet, in his earlier works, he also created miniature versions to explore the juxtaposition of scale and significance. These small sculptural pieces invite viewers to consider how size influences our understanding and appreciation of art. In this way, miniatures become a medium through which we can question societal norms and expectations.

The emotional connections we form with miniature objects cannot be overlooked. They often evoke memories of childhood, nostalgia for simpler times, or a sense of wonder. Think of a small toy figurine that once belonged to a beloved childhood playset. Holding it can transport you back to afternoons spent creating elaborate adventures, igniting feelings of joy and connection. These objects become a tangible link to our past, whispering stories of who we were and the moments that shaped us.

Moreover, miniatures provide a unique avenue for creativity and self-expression. The act of creating or collecting miniature objects allows individuals to explore their artistic inclinations. Model builders, for instance, meticulously construct miniature scenes that reflect their interests and passions. Whether it's a model of a historic building or a tiny fantasy landscape, each creation is a testament to the builder's vision and dedication. This process encourages attention to detail and fosters a sense of accomplishment as the final product comes to life.

In recent years, the popularity of miniature gardening has emerged as a delightful trend. Tiny plants, furniture, and figurines come together to create enchanting landscapes that inspire tranquility and creativity. These small gardens serve as personal retreats, inviting individuals to cultivate not only plants but also a sense of peace and mindfulness. The process of tending to a miniature garden allows for reflection and connection with nature, reminding us of the beauty that exists in both the grand and the small.

Furthermore, miniatures have found their place in the realm of therapy and well-being. Therapeutic practices increasingly recognize the value of engaging with small objects to promote mindfulness and relaxation. Activities such as miniature painting or assembling model kits can serve as a form of meditation, allowing individuals to immerse themselves in a focused, calming task. The repetitive nature of these activities can quiet the mind, offering solace in our fast-paced world. By engaging with miniatures, individuals can find a sense of grounding and presence.

Culturally, the fascination with miniatures is evident in various traditions. In countries like India, the art of miniature painting has flourished for centuries, showcasing intricate details and vibrant colors. These paintings often depict historical events, court scenes, or mythological tales, capturing the essence of a culture within a small canvas. The precision and skill required to create such detailed works demonstrate the deep appreciation for craftsmanship and storytelling that exists within miniature art forms.

In the digital age, the allure of miniatures has not waned. With the rise of social media platforms, enthusiasts from around the world share their collections and creations. Tiny worlds are showcased in stunning photographs, sparking inspiration and camaraderie among collectors and artists alike. Hashtags dedicated to miniature art allow individuals to connect, exchange ideas, and celebrate the joy of small things. This global community fosters a sense of belonging, uniting those who find beauty in the intricacies of miniatures.

The power of miniature objects lies in their ability to transcend mere aesthetics. They capture the essence of creativity, nostalgia, and human connection. Whether as tools for storytelling, expressions of artistry, or reminders of cherished memories, these small treasures hold immense significance. By embracing the beauty in the mundane, we open ourselves to a world of possibilities, reminding ourselves that even the tiniest objects can hold profound meaning. As we explore this realm of miniatures, we are invited to reflect on our own lives, finding joy and wonder in the little things that surround us. Ultimately, it is through these miniature objects that we can discover a larger narrative about ourselves and the world we inhabit.

Small Things in Different Cultures

Across the globe, small things resonate with profound meanings, often reflecting the values, beliefs, and histories of diverse cultures. These seemingly insignificant objects can carry immense weight, serving as symbols of identity, tradition, and connection. From tiny charms to delicate trinkets, the small things in various cultures often embody stories that link individuals to their heritage and provide insight into the human experience.

In Japan, the art of making netsuke illustrates the cultural significance of small objects. Originally designed as toggles for securing items on traditional clothing, these miniature carvings evolved into highly detailed works of art. Crafted from materials like wood, ivory, and even ceramic, netsuke depict a wide range of subjects, from animals to mythical creatures. Each piece is a testament to the artisan's skill and creativity, often carrying symbolic meanings. For instance, a netsuke featuring a turtle may represent longevity and wisdom, while one depicting a crane symbolizes good fortune. The appreciation for these small creations highlights the Japanese reverence for craftsmanship and the belief that beauty can be found in even the tiniest details.

Traveling to the Mediterranean, we encounter the tradition of the evil eye, or "nazar," in countries such as Turkey and Greece. These small, glass amulets are typically blue and white, designed to ward off negative energy and protect the wearer from harm. The nazar is not just a decorative object; it serves as a cultural talisman, embodying the collective belief in the power of protection. Families often hang them in their homes or wear them as jewelry, instilling a sense of safety and connection to their cultural heritage. The ubiquitous presence of the nazar in everyday life reflects how small objects can encapsulate shared beliefs and provide comfort amid uncertainties.

In India, the significance of small things can be observed in the tradition of gifting and exchanging "rakhi" during the festival of Raksha Bandhan. This festival celebrates the bond between brothers and sisters, and the rakhi—a decorative thread—serves as a symbol of protection and love. Sisters tie rakhis around their brothers' wrists, invoking blessings for their well-being, while brothers, in return, promise to protect their sisters. The rakhi may be simple or elaborately crafted, but its essence lies in the emotional connection it fosters. This small gesture encapsulates the deep-rooted familial bonds that permeate Indian culture, illustrating how a tiny object can carry immense emotional and cultural significance.

The Maori people of New Zealand also highlight the importance of small objects through their intricate carving traditions. The "pounamu," or greenstone, is often transformed into small pieces of jewelry or tools, each piece telling a story of lineage and ancestry. The carving of pounamu is steeped in cultural significance, as it connects the wearer to their heritage and the land. Each design is rich with symbolism, representing concepts such as strength, love, and protection. When gifted, these small objects signify deep respect and connection, reinforcing the idea that even the smallest items can carry the weight of history and identity.

In Africa, small artifacts such as beads play a vital role in cultural expression and social identity. Different tribes use beads in unique ways, often incorporating them into clothing, jewelry, and ceremonial items. For instance, the Maasai people of Kenya and Tanzania are renowned for their colorful beadwork, which serves not only as decoration but also as a means of communication. The colors and patterns convey information about age, marital status, and social standing. A single necklace can tell an intricate story about the wearer's life and background, demonstrating how small things can reflect complex social structures and cultural narratives.

Meanwhile, in the realm of storytelling, tiny books have emerged as a fascinating cultural phenomenon. In various societies, miniature books serve as both art and literature, showcasing the delicate balance between craftsmanship and storytelling. Artists and writers create these small volumes to capture poetry, prose, or illustrations, often exploring themes of nature, love, and identity. These tiny tomes invite readers to engage with literature in a unique way, fostering a sense of intimacy and reflection. The existence of miniature books across cultures signifies a shared appreciation for storytelling, regardless of geographical boundaries.

In the realm of culinary traditions, small items such as spices and condiments reveal the rich tapestry of cultural practices. For example, in Indian cuisine, the use of small spices like cumin, cardamom, and turmeric is foundational. Each spice carries its own history and significance, often intertwined with ancient trade routes and cultural exchanges. The careful selection and blending of these spices showcase the depth of Indian culinary art, where even the smallest ingredient can transform a dish into a masterpiece. Similarly, the use of small herbs in Mediterranean cooking, such as basil or oregano, enhances flavors and reflects regional agricultural practices, highlighting the connection between food, culture, and identity.

Exploring the significance of small things in different cultures offers a glimpse into the shared human experience. These objects, often overlooked in the hustle and bustle of modern life, serve as reminders of our connections to history, community, and identity. They encapsulate stories that transcend time and geography, illustrating how small items can evoke powerful emotions and foster a sense of belonging. Whether it's through the craftsmanship of netsuke, the protective powers of the nazar, or the familial bonds symbolized by rakhi, these tiny artifacts reveal the rich layers of meaning that can be found in the simplest of things.

As we navigate a world that often emphasizes the grand and the extraordinary, it is essential to recognize the beauty and significance of the small. By appreciating these miniature treasures, we can cultivate a deeper understanding of the diverse cultures that shape our lives. In the end, it is the small things that connect us all, reminding us of our shared humanity and the stories that bind us together across time and space.

Symbolism and Meaning in Collectibles

Collectibles hold a unique place in the tapestry of human experience, transcending mere objects to embody stories, memories, and emotions. From vintage toys to rare stamps, every collectible is imbued with symbolism and meaning that can reveal much about the collector and the culture from which the item originates. This intricate relationship between the object and its significance can be dissected through various lenses, including nostalgia, identity, and the interplay of value and desirability.

Nostalgia often plays a pivotal role in the allure of collectibles. Many enthusiasts are drawn to items that evoke memories of their past—perhaps a childhood toy, a comic book, or a piece of memorabilia from a beloved film. These artifacts serve as tangible connections to simpler times, providing comfort and sparking joyful reminiscence. For instance, a collector who seeks out action figures from their youth may be trying to recapture the wonder and excitement they felt as a child. This yearning for the past is not merely about possession; it's about the emotional resonance these items carry. The act of collecting becomes a journey through one's personal history, where each item represents a fragment of a cherished memory.

The symbolism of collectibles can also be deeply intertwined with identity. For many, the items they choose to collect reflect their interests, passions, and affiliations. A person who collects vinyl records may be expressing a love for music and a connection to the counterculture movements of the past. Similarly, someone who amasses vintage clothing might be celebrating unique fashion trends and embracing a style that sets them apart from the mainstream. In this way, collectibles become extensions of the self, allowing individuals to define and communicate their identities to the world. The choices made in collecting can signify values, beliefs, and even social status, creating a rich narrative that goes far beyond the physical object itself.

The significance of collectibles often transcends individual identity, tapping into broader cultural narratives. Items like baseball cards or limited-edition sneakers can embody the spirit of a generation or a cultural movement. For example, the rise of sneaker culture speaks to the intersection of fashion, sport, and urban identity. Sneakers that were once mere athletic gear have transformed into coveted collector's items, with certain pairs fetching astronomical prices at auctions. This phenomenon illustrates how collectibles can symbolize cultural shifts and societal values, reflecting trends that resonate with a community.

Moreover, the value of collectibles is often influenced by the interplay of rarity and desirability. A limited-edition item, whether it's a piece of art or a comic book, draws interest not only for its aesthetics but also for its exclusivity. Collectors are often motivated by the thrill of the hunt, searching for items that are difficult to find and may appreciate in value over time. This is particularly evident in the world of fine art, where works by renowned artists are sought after not just for their beauty but for their investment potential. The symbolism of these items is layered—each piece becomes a status symbol, representing both financial acumen and a deep appreciation for artistry.

The narrative surrounding collectibles can shift dramatically based on their provenance. An item with a rich history or a notable previous owner often carries more weight than an otherwise similar piece without such a background. For example, a watch worn by a famous athlete or a guitar once owned by a legendary musician can transform into a cultural artifact, laden with stories and significance. The symbolism here extends beyond the object itself to encompass the legacy of the individuals associated with it, enhancing its allure for collectors.

Collectibles also serve as a means of preserving history and culture. Museums and private collectors alike recognize the importance of safeguarding artifacts that capture significant moments, traditions, and innovations. Items such as vintage postcards, historical documents, and traditional crafts provide insights into past societies, enabling future generations to understand cultural evolution. In this context, collectibles become vessels of memory, preserving narratives that might otherwise fade into obscurity. The act of collecting, therefore, takes on a communal dimension, as individuals contribute to the collective memory of their culture.

The emotional connection to collectibles can also lead to a sense of community among enthusiasts. Collectors often gather at conventions, online forums, and social media groups to share their passions, trade items, and recount stories. This social aspect of collecting fosters camaraderie, as individuals bond over shared interests and experiences. The symbolism of collectibles is heightened in these spaces, as they represent not just personal passions but also connections with others who appreciate the same items. This sense of belonging can be a powerful motivator, encouraging collectors to engage more deeply with their pursuits.

Additionally, the practice of collecting can serve as a form of artistic expression. Many collectors take pride in curating their collections, arranging items in visually appealing ways that tell a story or showcase a theme. This artistic approach transforms the act of collecting into a creative endeavor, where the arrangement and presentation of items become an art form in itself. Whether displayed in a home or shared online, these collections invite viewers to engage with the symbolism and meaning behind each piece, sparking conversations about taste, culture, and personal history.

As we delve into the world of collectibles, it becomes clear that their significance extends far beyond their physical presence. Each item carries a wealth of symbolism and meaning, shaped by individual experiences, cultural narratives, and societal values. Collectibles connect us to our past, define aspects of our identities, and foster community among like-minded enthusiasts. They serve as reminders that even the smallest objects can hold immense power, capable of evoking emotions, preserving history, and creating shared experiences. In a world that often prioritizes the new and the flashy, the enduring appeal of collectibles invites us to reflect on the beauty and significance of the stories they tell.

How Small Objects Shape Our Lives

Small objects often slip under the radar of our daily lives, yet their impact can be profound and far-reaching. These seemingly insignificant items, from keys and coins to trinkets and tools, weave through our routines, influencing our emotions, interactions, and memories. They possess the power to shape our experiences in subtle yet significant ways, acting as anchors in the ever-changing tide of life.

Consider the keychain that jangles in your pocket. It holds not just keys but also memories and emotions tied to the spaces they unlock. Each key can represent a chapter of your life—a home, a car, a cherished place that holds significance. The act of reaching for your keys can trigger a flood of memories, transporting you back to moments spent in those spaces. This tiny collection of metal not only provides access but also serves as a tangible reminder of the places you've inhabited and the experiences you've gathered along the way.

Similarly, the coins that accumulate in your purse or on the kitchen counter often carry stories of their own. Each coin can symbolize transactions made, places visited, or experiences shared. A quarter from a trip to a bustling market might remind you of the laughter shared with friends as you bartered for trinkets, while a penny found on the street could evoke thoughts of luck and serendipity. These small pieces of currency act as vessels for our memories, linking us to moments both mundane and extraordinary.

The role of small objects extends to the emotional landscape of our lives. A simple token, like a friendship bracelet or a locket, can encapsulate deep feelings and connections. These items often carry the weight of relationships, symbolizing love, loyalty, or shared experiences. For instance, a bracelet woven from colorful threads may remind you of the summer spent with a dear friend, filled with laughter and adventures. Each time you glance at it, you are reminded of that bond, reinforcing the importance of relationships that shape who you are.

Small objects also serve as catalysts for creativity and inspiration. An artist might keep a collection of buttons, shells, or stones—each one a potential source of artistic expression. These items, while small and often overlooked, can spark ideas and fuel the creative process. A button might inspire a new design, while a unique stone could lead to a sculpture. The act of collecting and arranging these diminutive treasures encourages exploration and experimentation, showcasing how the smallest items can lead to the grandest of ideas.

In the realm of personal organization, small objects play a crucial role in shaping our habits and productivity. Think of the notepad that sits on your desk, filled with reminders, ideas, and to-do lists. This simple object serves as a lifeline in our fast-paced lives, helping to structure our thoughts and tasks. The act of writing down goals or reminders can provide clarity and focus, shaping how we navigate our days. Similarly, items like planners or sticky notes can create a sense of order in an otherwise chaotic world, proving that even small organizational tools can have a monumental impact on our efficiency and mindset.

The influence of small objects can also extend into the social realm. Consider the importance of gifts—often small tokens of appreciation or love. A handwritten note, a small plant, or a simple piece of jewelry can convey messages of care and thoughtfulness. These items symbolize connection and intention, serving to strengthen bonds between individuals. The act of giving and receiving small gifts creates an emotional exchange that fosters relationships, illustrating how a seemingly minor object can carry immense significance.

Cultural artifacts provide another layer of understanding regarding the impact of small objects. Items like traditional dolls, miniature sculptures, or religious symbols can encapsulate the values and beliefs of a culture. A small figurine representing a deity can serve as a focal point for spiritual reflection, while a handcrafted ornament may embody the craftsmanship and history of a particular community. These objects connect individuals to their cultural roots, shaping their identities and providing a sense of belonging. In this way, small items act as conduits for cultural heritage, bridging the past and present.

Even in the digital age, small objects continue to shape our lives in unique ways. Consider the smartphone, a device that fits comfortably in the palm of your hand yet serves as a gateway to the world. It holds memories in the form of photos, connects us with loved ones across distances, and provides access to a wealth of information. This small object has revolutionized communication, reshaping how we interact with one another and the world around us. As we carry our devices with us, we also carry the influence of technology on our social dynamics, personal relationships, and even our self-perception.

The significance of small objects can also be seen in the realm of mindfulness and well-being. Items like worry stones or fidget spinners provide tangible ways to manage stress and anxiety. These small tools offer comfort, allowing individuals to engage in calming behaviors that promote mental health. The act of holding or manipulating these objects can provide a sense of grounding, illustrating how even the simplest items can contribute to emotional balance and self-care.

As we navigate through life, it becomes increasingly apparent that small objects shape our existence in multifaceted ways. They serve as reminders of our past, catalysts for creativity, and symbols of connection. In a world that often emphasizes the grand and the extraordinary, it is essential to recognize the profound impact of the small. By appreciating these diminutive treasures, we can cultivate a deeper understanding of how they influence our experiences and shape our identities. Ultimately, it is through the lens of these small objects that we can gain insight into the intricate tapestry of our lives, revealing the beauty and significance that can be found in the everyday.

Chapter 3: Paperclips A Closer Look

The History of the Paperclip

The paperclip, often regarded as a mundane office supply, has a rich and intriguing history that reflects broader themes of innovation, design, and practicality. This simple yet effective tool has not only organized our documents but has also woven itself into the fabric of everyday life, transcending its original purpose to symbolize cleverness and versatility.

The origins of the paperclip can be traced back to the late 19th century, a time when the industrial revolution was in full swing, and the demand for efficient office supplies was rising. The first recorded patent for a paperclip was granted to Samuel B. Fay in 1867. However, Fay's design was rather complex and not particularly successful in practical use. It featured a unique mechanism that allowed it to bind papers together, but it lacked the simplicity and ease of use that characterized future designs.

It wasn't until 1899 that the paperclip as we know it began to take shape. The invention attributed to this pivotal moment is the Gem paperclip, created by the Gem Manufacturing Company in Britain. The design was deceptively simple—a single piece of wire bent into a distinctive shape—yet it revolutionized the way papers were held together. Its elegant form allowed for easy insertion and removal without causing damage to the documents, making it an instant favorite among clerks and office workers.

What made the Gem paperclip particularly remarkable was its ability to adapt to various uses beyond merely holding papers together. Its shape allowed it to function as a bookmark, a zipper pull, or even a makeshift tool for resetting electronic devices. This versatility contributed to its widespread adoption and ensured its place in offices and homes around the world. In a rapidly industrializing society, where efficiency was paramount, the paperclip emerged as a symbol of ingenuity and practicality.

During World War II, the paperclip took on a new and profound significance. In Norway, where the Nazi regime had occupied the country, citizens began wearing paperclips on their lapels as a silent form of resistance. The act symbolized solidarity and unity against oppression, turning a simple office supply into a powerful emblem of defiance. This poignant use of the paperclip highlights how everyday objects can adopt new meanings in the context of social and political movements, illustrating the profound connection between material culture and human experience.

The design of the paperclip has remained relatively unchanged since its inception, a testament to its effectiveness. While many variations and adaptations have emerged, the basic form has endured. Some designs, such as the triangular and spiral paperclips, have attempted to enhance functionality or aesthetics, but none have eclipsed the original Gem paperclip in popularity. Its unpretentious elegance and straightforward utility have made it a staple in offices, schools, and homes, serving as a reminder that simplicity can often yield the most effective solutions.

The production of paperclips has evolved alongside technological advancements. Initially crafted by hand, the manufacturing process became increasingly automated in the 20th century, allowing for mass production. Today, machines produce millions of paperclips each day, ensuring that this essential item remains readily available to consumers around the globe. The efficient manufacturing processes reflect broader trends in industrial design, where optimizing production while maintaining quality has become a hallmark of modern manufacturing.

Interestingly, the paperclip has also made its mark in the world of art and design. Artists and designers have embraced the paperclip's form, incorporating it into sculptures, installations, and creative projects. Its simple geometry lends itself to exploration, encouraging artists to reimagine its use and significance. This artistic reinterpretation underscores the idea that even the most unassuming objects can inspire creativity and innovation.

Moreover, the rise of digital technology has led to speculation about the future of the paperclip. As offices become increasingly paperless, one might wonder whether this humble tool will fade into obscurity. However, the paperclip remains relevant even in a digital age. Its ability to organize physical documents continues to be valued, especially in environments where printed materials are still utilized. Additionally, the paperclip's enduring popularity serves as a reminder of the tactile experience of handling physical objects in an increasingly virtual world.

The paperclip's journey is a testament to human ingenuity and the power of simple design. It has evolved from a modest invention into a symbol of resistance and resilience. The way it has been adopted, adapted, and embraced by different cultures speaks to its universal appeal. What began as a practical solution to a common problem has transformed into an object imbued with meaning, creativity, and history.

In reflecting on the paperclip's story, one cannot help but appreciate the beauty of small objects and their ability to shape our lives in unexpected ways. The next time you reach for a paperclip, take a moment to consider its journey—a journey that intertwines practicality with symbolism, creativity with resistance. This seemingly ordinary object encapsulates the essence of innovation and serves as a reminder that even the simplest designs can leave an indelible mark on the world.

Varieties of Paperclips

The world of paperclips is surprisingly diverse, with a range of designs that cater to various needs and preferences. While the classic Gem paperclip remains the most recognized, the evolution of this simple tool has given rise to a plethora of varieties, each with its own unique features and applications. Understanding these different types opens a window into the creativity and practicality behind such a humble yet essential object.

The classic Gem paperclip is a staple in offices and homes alike, known for its elegant, streamlined design. It consists of a single wire bent into a loop, allowing it to hold multiple sheets of paper securely without causing damage. This design is not just aesthetically pleasing; it is functional, providing ease of use and efficiency. However, as the needs of users evolved, so did the designs of paperclips.

One popular alternative is the triangular paperclip. This version utilizes three points to grip the paper, providing a more secure hold compared to its round counterpart. Ideal for thicker stacks of paper, the triangular design ensures that documents remain fastened without the risk of slipping. Its unique shape also lends a touch of visual interest, making it a favorite among those who appreciate a little flair in their office supplies.

The spiral paperclip offers yet another twist on the traditional design. Featuring a spiral shape, this type provides a strong grasp on papers, making it particularly useful for organizing loose sheets. Its unique form allows for a more flexible approach to binding documents, accommodating varying thicknesses with ease. While it may not be as commonly found as the Gem, the spiral paperclip is a testament to the innovative spirit that drives the development of office supplies.

For those seeking a more robust solution, the bulldog clip stands out as a powerful alternative. Unlike traditional paperclips, bulldog clips feature a spring-loaded mechanism that allows them to clamp down on papers securely. They are perfect for holding together large volumes of documents, making them a preferred choice in environments where organization is paramount. The simplicity of the bulldog clip's design, combined with its strength, makes it a versatile tool in any workspace.

Beyond these functional variations, decorative paperclips have also gained popularity. These clips come in an array of colors, shapes, and sizes, transforming a standard office supply into a fun and expressive accessory. From whimsical designs shaped like animals to elegant floral patterns, decorative paperclips allow users to personalize their workspace. They serve not only as practical tools but also as a means of self-expression, bringing a bit of joy to the mundane task of organizing paperwork.

In recent years, magnetic paperclips have emerged as a modern alternative. Utilizing magnets instead of a traditional clasp, these clips offer the advantage of easy attachment and removal. They are particularly useful for securing documents in a way that avoids damage, as there is no pressure applied to the paper. Magnetic paperclips are also great for holding together papers while still allowing for easy access, making them an appealing option for those who prioritize convenience.

Another innovative design is the binder clip, which combines the principles of the traditional paperclip with the strength of a bulldog clip. Made of a rectangular base with two metal arms, binder clips can hold large quantities of paper together, making them ideal for presentations or reports. Their hinged design allows for easy opening and closing, ensuring that documents can be added or removed without hassle. The binder clip's capability to hold thick stacks of paper securely makes it a staple in many workplaces.

The versatility of paperclips extends to their size variations as well. Mini paperclips are often used for lighter tasks, such as securing a few pages together or marking a place in a book. Their smaller size is ideal for lightweight documents, ensuring that they don't overwhelm the pages they are holding. Conversely, jumbo paperclips are designed for heavier tasks, accommodating thicker documents or larger groups of papers with ease. This range of sizes allows users to select the appropriate clip for their specific needs, enhancing efficiency and organization.

Even within the realm of specialty paperclips, unique designs cater to niche markets. For example, some paperclips are designed with built-in index tabs, allowing users to label and organize documents easily. Others may come in the form of shapes relevant to specific industries, such as music notes for music teachers or gears for engineering firms. This customization adds an extra layer of functionality, proving that even a simple object like a paperclip can be tailored to suit specific purposes.

The environmental impact of paperclips is also worth noting. As sustainability becomes increasingly important, some manufacturers have begun producing eco-friendly paperclips made from recycled materials. These clips serve the dual purpose of providing organization while also minimizing waste, appealing to consumers who prioritize environmentally responsible choices. The evolution of paperclips continues to reflect broader trends in society, showcasing the interplay between practicality and ecological consciousness.

The plethora of paperclip varieties demonstrates that even the most ordinary objects can be reimagined and reinvented. From the classic Gem paperclip to innovative designs like magnetic clips and binder clips, each type serves a distinct purpose while reflecting the creativity of its designers. The adaptability of these small tools allows them to fit seamlessly into our lives, providing solutions to everyday challenges while adding a touch of individuality to our workspaces.

As we navigate the complexities of modern life, the humble paperclip remains a reliable companion, embodying the values of simplicity and efficiency. The next time you reach for one, consider the vast array of options available—each variation not only serves a practical function but also tells a story about human ingenuity and the desire to improve everyday experiences. In a world filled with technological advancements, the enduring charm of the paperclip reminds us of the beauty of simplicity and the importance of thoughtful design.

The Design Evolution of Paperclips

The evolution of the paperclip is a fascinating journey through time, reflecting broader trends in design, functionality, and the changing needs of society. This simple tool, often overlooked in the grand scheme of office supplies, has undergone significant transformations that speak to human ingenuity and the quest for efficiency.

The story begins in the late 19th century when the demand for effective document management surged alongside the rise of businesses and bureaucracies. The initial designs of paperclips were often cumbersome and not particularly user-friendly. Samuel B. Fay's patent in 1867 featured a complex mechanism intended to hold papers together, but it failed to gain traction. The design was more intricate than necessary, and its practicality was limited. It wasn't until 1899 that a turning point occurred with the introduction of the Gem paperclip, a design that would set the standard for decades to come.

The Gem paperclip, with its elegant and functional design, is a study in simplicity. Crafted from a single wire bent into a loop, it allows for the easy attachment and detachment of papers without causing damage. This approach to design—prioritizing functionality while maintaining a clean aesthetic—has influenced countless products since. The genius of the Gem paperclip lies in its ability to hold together multiple sheets of paper securely, while also being easy to remove, a characteristic that makes it indispensable in offices worldwide.

As the 20th century unfolded, the world witnessed a series of innovations that further refined the paperclip's design. Variations began to emerge, each tailored to specific needs. Triangular paperclips entered the market, offering a more secure grip for thicker stacks of documents. Their geometric shape appealed to those who required a reliable solution for managing larger volumes of paper. This adaptability reflected a growing understanding of user needs and a shift towards designs that catered to a wider audience.

The production processes for paperclips also evolved during this time. Originally crafted by hand, the manufacturing of paperclips became increasingly automated, allowing for mass production. This transformation exemplified the broader trends of the industrial age, where efficiency and scalability were paramount. As machines took over, the quality and availability of paperclips improved dramatically, ensuring that this essential office supply remained accessible to everyone.

The mid-20th century marked another significant phase in the design evolution of paperclips. With the advent of new materials and manufacturing techniques, designers began experimenting with different forms and functionalities. Spirals and decorative shapes emerged, showcasing creativity while still retaining the core purpose of binding papers together. The spiral paperclip, for instance, provided flexibility, accommodating various paper thicknesses while adding an element of visual interest. These innovations highlighted the balance between artistic expression and practical utility.

During this period, the paperclip also began to take on symbolic meanings. In Norway during World War II, citizens wore paperclips as a silent act of resistance against Nazi occupation. This simple object, usually associated with organization, transformed into a powerful emblem of solidarity and defiance. This instance illustrates how design can transcend functionality and enter the realm of social and political significance, showcasing the profound impact that even the smallest objects can have on human experience.

As the 21st century approached, the digital revolution began to cast a shadow over traditional office supplies. With the rise of electronic communication and paperless offices, many wondered about the future of the paperclip. Yet, instead of fading into obscurity, the paperclip adapted once again. New variations emerged, such as magnetic paperclips, which offered an easy and non-damaging way to hold documents together. These modern designs retained the essence of the original paperclip while embracing advancements in technology.

Sustainability became a crucial consideration in the design and production of paperclips as environmental awareness grew. Manufacturers began producing clips from recycled materials, addressing the increasing demand for eco-friendly office supplies. This shift not only reflects changing consumer preferences but also demonstrates how design evolution is influenced by societal values and the need for responsible consumption.

The decorative paperclip trend flourished in recent years, providing a means for personalization in an otherwise utilitarian workspace. With vibrant colors, unique shapes, and artistic designs, decorative paperclips allow individuals to express their personalities while organizing their documents. This playful approach to design emphasizes the idea that even practical items can bring joy and creativity to everyday tasks.

The binder clip emerged as another evolution of the paperclip, combining the principles of the classic design with enhanced functionality. Its robust construction and adjustable clamps made it particularly suitable for holding larger groups of papers. This design evolution illustrates a keen understanding of user needs in diverse environments, from offices to classrooms, as people constantly seek effective solutions for organization.

The ongoing evolution of paperclips serves as a reminder that even the simplest objects can undergo remarkable transformations. Each design iteration reflects a response to changing societal needs, technological advancements, and aesthetic preferences. The enduring popularity of paperclips, despite the rise of digital alternatives, underscores their fundamental role in our lives. They remind us of the value of simplicity in design and the importance of practical solutions.

As we continue to innovate and adapt in an ever-changing world, the humble paperclip stands as a testament to the power of thoughtful design. Its journey from a basic tool to a multifaceted symbol of creativity, resistance, and organization encapsulates the essence of human ingenuity. The next time you reach for a paperclip, consider the rich history and evolution that have shaped this unassuming object, and appreciate the myriad ways it continues to enhance our daily lives.

Unusual Uses for Paperclips

The paperclip, a seemingly mundane office supply, is often taken for granted as a simple tool for holding sheets of paper together. Yet, its versatility extends far beyond its primary function. This unassuming little object has found a place in various unexpected scenarios, showcasing creativity and resourcefulness. When faced with challenges, many have turned to the paperclip, discovering innovative uses that transform it from a mere organizational tool into a multifunctional asset.

One of the most well-known alternative uses for paperclips is as a makeshift SIM card ejector. In our increasingly mobile world, accessing the SIM card slot on a phone can sometimes be a challenge, especially when the proper tool is not available. A standard paperclip, when straightened out just a bit, can easily fit into the tiny hole, allowing you to pop out the SIM card tray. This clever solution highlights how a simple design can serve multiple purposes, particularly in moments of need.

Beyond technology, the paperclip has also proven its worth in the realm of crafting. Crafters often utilize paperclips as connectors or fasteners for various projects. For example, they can be transformed into unique jewelry pieces, forming the basis for earrings or bracelets. By bending and twisting paperclips, one can create intricate designs that capture attention and showcase personal style. This creative application not only repurposes the paperclip but also brings a sense of individuality to the wearer.

In the kitchen, a paperclip can come to the rescue in various ways. It can be employed to seal snack bags, ensuring that chips or other treats stay fresh once opened. Simply twist the paperclip around the opening of the bag to create a secure closure. This makeshift solution is particularly handy when one finds themselves without a proper bag clip. Additionally, paperclips can be used to hold recipes or notes in place on the kitchen counter, preventing them from blowing away while cooking.

Travelers often find themselves in need of quick fixes, and the paperclip is a trusty companion. For instance, if a zipper on a bag or piece of clothing malfunctions, a paperclip can serve as a temporary zipper pull. By attaching the paperclip to the zipper tab, you can continue to use the item until a more permanent solution is available. This adaptability makes the paperclip an essential item in any travel kit, ready to assist in unforeseen circumstances.

In the realm of organization, paperclips can help keep life more manageable in surprising ways. They can be used as bookmarks, allowing readers to easily mark their page without damaging the book. Simply slip a paperclip onto the desired page, and you have a simple, effective way to pick up right where you left off. Similarly, paperclips can function as labels or dividers in files, helping to categorize documents without the need for more elaborate systems.

For those who enjoy DIY projects, the paperclip can be transformed into tools for various tasks. It can serve as a mini screwdriver, particularly for small screws in eyeglasses or electronics. By bending the end of a paperclip into a small hook, you can use it to tighten or loosen screws with precision. This makeshift tool can be invaluable in situations where the proper screwdriver is not at hand, showcasing the paperclip's ability to adapt to specific needs.

Another surprising use for paperclips is in the realm of technology and electronics. When working with small devices, such as computer peripherals or gaming controllers, a paperclip can be used to reset devices. Many gadgets have tiny reset buttons that are difficult to press without a pointed object. A paperclip, when unfolded, fits perfectly into these small spaces, allowing for easy access to reset functions. This simple trick can save time and frustration, making the paperclip an indispensable tool in tech maintenance.

The utility of paperclips extends even to home repairs. They can be used to temporarily hold together pieces of furniture or to create makeshift hooks for hanging items. For example, if a picture frame's hanging mechanism breaks, a paperclip can be fashioned into a hook that serves the same purpose until a more permanent fix is found. This ability to adapt to different scenarios illustrates the ingenuity that can arise from using everyday objects in unconventional ways.

In educational settings, teachers and students alike have found innovative uses for paperclips. Students can utilize them to create models or prototypes for science projects, showcasing their creativity while learning about structural integrity. Teachers might use paperclips to organize classroom materials or even as teaching aids, demonstrating concepts such as loops, connections, and even basic geometry. This educational versatility reaffirms the paperclip's role as more than just a tool for holding papers.

The world of fashion has also seen the paperclip make a surprising appearance. Fashion designers have incorporated paperclips into runway looks, using them as embellishments on clothing or accessories. This unexpected use challenges traditional norms of fashion, turning a simple office supply into a statement piece. The juxtaposition of elegance and utility speaks to a broader trend of repurposing everyday items in the fashion industry, bridging the gap between practicality and style.

As the paperclip continues to find new life in various domains, it serves as a reminder of the potential hidden within everyday objects. Its adaptability and resourcefulness inspire creativity, encouraging individuals to think outside the box. Whether it's in the kitchen, at work, or during travel, the paperclip proves time and again that it can rise to the occasion, providing solutions in unexpected ways.

Embracing the unusual uses of the paperclip not only highlights the importance of creativity and resourcefulness but also encourages a mindset of innovation. This simple tool, with its humble origins, has transcended its primary function, becoming a symbol of ingenuity. So, the next time you find yourself in need, consider reaching for a paperclip. Its potential is limited only by one's imagination, reminding us that even the most ordinary objects can serve extraordinary purposes.

The Paperclip in Popular Culture

The paperclip, often dismissed as a mere functional object, has carved out an intriguing niche in popular culture. Its unassuming presence belies a rich tapestry of meanings and representations that extend far beyond the confines of the office. From art and literature to film and music, this simple tool has captured the imagination of creators and audiences alike, symbolizing everything from organization and efficiency to creativity and rebellion.

In the realm of literature, the paperclip has made notable appearances, often serving as a metaphor for simplicity or the mundane aspects of life. Writers have utilized it to illustrate character traits or to enhance themes of order and chaos. In a story where a character is overwhelmed by the complexities of life, the humble paperclip can symbolize a desire for simplicity and structure. This subtle yet powerful representation resonates with readers, evoking a sense of nostalgia for the uncomplicated elements of daily existence.

Visual artists have also found inspiration in the paperclip. Its unique shape and form lend themselves to creative interpretations. Some contemporary artists incorporate paperclips into their works, using them as tools for sculpture or as part of mixed media pieces. The juxtaposition of a common office supply with high art challenges traditional boundaries, inviting viewers to reconsider their perceptions of both art and the objects that surround them. This use of the paperclip as a material reflects a broader trend in art, where everyday items are transformed into thought-provoking statements.

In film and television, the paperclip has occasionally taken on a life of its own, becoming a symbol of ingenuity and resourcefulness. Iconic scenes often depict characters using paperclips in clever ways to solve problems or escape tricky situations. For instance, a protagonist might use a paperclip to pick a lock, showcasing not only their quick thinking but also the versatile nature of this simple tool. Such moments resonate with audiences, reinforcing the idea that creativity can emerge from the most unexpected sources.

The paperclip has also found its way into the realm of music. Songwriters and musicians have referenced it in lyrics, using it as a metaphor for connection and organization in relationships or life experiences. A song may evoke the image of a paperclip to symbolize the bonds that hold people together, reflecting themes of intimacy and support. This imagery captures the essence of how everyday objects can embody deeper meanings, adding layers to the storytelling in music.

Beyond individual works of art and media, the paperclip has become part of broader cultural conversations, particularly regarding its role in technology and innovation. In an era increasingly defined by digital communication, the paperclip serves as a nostalgic reminder of a time when physical documents were the norm. The transition from paper to screens has sparked discussions about the relevance of traditional office supplies, and the paperclip often emerges as a symbol of resilience in a changing world. It represents both a bygone era and a continuing need for simple solutions, bridging the gap between the past and present.

Moreover, the paperclip's role as a symbol of rebellion and resistance cannot be overlooked. During World War II, Norwegians adopted the paperclip as a covert symbol of defiance against the Nazi occupation. Citizens wore paperclips on their clothing as a silent protest, demonstrating unity and resilience in the face of oppression. This powerful act of solidarity transformed a simple object into a profound emblem of hope and resistance, showcasing the ability of everyday items to carry significant weight in times of struggle.

In the realm of design and innovation, the paperclip has also inspired countless creative endeavors. Designers have reimagined the paperclip in various forms, creating jewelry, home decor, and even fashion accessories that pay homage to its iconic shape. These products often celebrate the beauty of simplicity, reminding us that even the most ordinary objects can be reinterpreted into something extraordinary. This trend reflects a growing appreciation for minimalism and functional design in contemporary culture.

The paperclip's presence in social media and online culture further exemplifies its relevance in today's society. Memes and humorous posts often reference the paperclip as a metaphor for everyday life, encapsulating the struggles and triumphs of modern existence. Whether it is a joke about the frustrations of office work or a clever commentary on organization, the paperclip continues to resonate with people across various platforms, cementing its status as a cultural icon.

As we navigate a world filled with constant change and innovation, the paperclip endures as a symbol of practicality and simplicity. Its ability to adapt and find relevance in diverse contexts speaks to the power of everyday objects to connect us to our shared experiences. The paperclip serves as a reminder that, despite the complexities of life, there is beauty in simplicity and utility.

This small yet mighty object has woven itself into the fabric of our culture, embodying creativity, resilience, and ingenuity. Whether it appears in a heartfelt song, a poignant piece of art, or a clever film scene, the paperclip's influence is undeniable. It challenges us to view the ordinary in extraordinary ways, encouraging us to appreciate the small things that shape our lives. Through its various representations in popular culture, the paperclip stands as a testament to the enduring nature of simple ideas and the profound impact they can have on our collective imagination.

Chapter 4: Organizing Your Collection

Display Techniques for Small Items

Showcasing small items can be both an art and a science, requiring a keen eye for design and an understanding of how to make the most of limited space. Whether it's a collection of miniature figurines, jewelry, or office supplies, the right display techniques can transform these objects into captivating focal points that draw attention and admiration. The goal is to create a visually appealing arrangement that enhances the items' intrinsic qualities while also telling a story about their significance.

One of the most effective ways to display small items is through the use of layering. This technique involves arranging objects at varying heights and depths to create a sense of dimension. For example, when displaying a collection of antique thimbles, placing them on a tiered stand allows each piece to be seen clearly while adding a dynamic quality to the arrangement. Layering can be achieved using various materials—stacked boxes, risers, or even natural elements like stones or logs can elevate certain pieces, making them more prominent.

Color coordination plays a crucial role in the visual impact of a display. Grouping small items by color can create a cohesive look that is pleasing to the eye. Imagine a collection of vintage buttons arranged in a gradient from deep reds to soft pastels. Such a display not only highlights the beauty of each button but also creates an overall sense of harmony. Alternatively, contrasting colors can be used to create striking displays that capture attention. A bright turquoise vase filled with white flowers against a dark background makes both the vase and the flowers pop, making them the centerpiece of the arrangement.

Lighting is another critical factor to consider when displaying small items. Proper illumination can dramatically enhance the appearance of objects, revealing their textures and colors in a way that natural light alone cannot. Soft, diffused lighting can create an inviting atmosphere, while focused spotlights can draw attention to specific items, such as a treasured heirloom or a piece of artwork. Utilizing display cases with built-in lighting can add an extra layer of elegance, allowing collectors to showcase their items while keeping them protected from dust and damage.

Incorporating thematic elements into a display can also add depth and context. For instance, if you're showcasing a collection of seashells, consider using a sand-colored base, adding beach-related items like small driftwood pieces or photos from seaside vacations. This approach not only highlights the shells but also tells a story about their origins, evoking memories of sunny days by the ocean. Themes can also be seasonal; displaying small pumpkins, gourds, and autumn leaves during the fall creates a festive atmosphere that resonates with the spirit of the season.

The choice of containers or display vessels can significantly influence the overall effect of a presentation. Clear glass jars, bowls, or cloches can provide a clean, minimalist way to display small items while allowing viewers to appreciate their details. For example, a collection of colorful marbles can be beautifully showcased in a simple glass bowl, creating a stunning centerpiece. On the other hand, textured or decorative containers can enhance the charm of the objects within. A rustic wooden box can add warmth to a display of vintage postcards, inviting viewers to explore the contents.

Creating a narrative through arrangement is another powerful technique. Instead of simply placing items randomly, think about how they can interact with one another. A small figurine can be positioned next to a book that features a story about that character, prompting questions and evoking curiosity. This storytelling approach engages viewers, encouraging them to look closer and discover the connections between the items. A well-curated display can often lead to meaningful conversations, as people share their interpretations and experiences related to the items.

Utilizing negative space is a concept often overlooked in display design. By allowing for empty space around objects, you can draw attention to the items themselves. A single, beautifully crafted ceramic piece displayed against a neutral backdrop creates a striking visual impact. Negative space helps to prevent clutter, giving each item room to breathe and allowing viewers to focus on the details without overwhelming their senses. It also encourages a more thoughtful appreciation of each piece, fostering a deeper connection between the viewer and the displayed items.

The arrangement of small items can also benefit from the principles of balance and symmetry. Symmetrical displays tend to create a sense of order and calm, making them particularly effective in settings where a tranquil atmosphere is desired. In contrast, asymmetrical arrangements can evoke a more dynamic and energetic feel. For example, placing larger items on one side while balancing them with several smaller pieces on the other can create an engaging visual tension. This interplay between balance and movement invites viewers to explore the display, discovering its nuances.

Incorporating interactive elements can enhance the viewing experience, especially for displays in public spaces or homes with children. Allowing people to touch or rearrange items can foster a sense of connection and engagement. For instance, a display of small art supplies, such as colored pencils and sketchbooks, invites creativity, encouraging users to pick up a pencil and start drawing. Interactive displays can turn passive viewers into active participants, enriching their experience and making the items more memorable.

Finally, regular rotation of displayed items keeps the arrangement fresh and exciting. Changing displays seasonally or thematically can not only maintain interest but also provide opportunities to showcase new acquisitions or highlight different aspects of a collection. This practice encourages ongoing interaction with the items, allowing them to continue telling their stories in new contexts.

The art of displaying small items is a multifaceted endeavor that blends creativity, organization, and storytelling. By employing techniques such as layering, color coordination, and thematic elements, one can transform everyday objects into striking displays that capture attention and inspire appreciation. Through thoughtful arrangement and consideration of lighting, negative space, and interactivity, small items can be elevated from obscurity to prominence, inviting viewers to explore and engage with their charm. Whether in a personal space or a public exhibition, effective display techniques breathe life into small items, celebrating their beauty and significance in our lives.

Cataloging and Inventory

Maintaining an organized cataloging and inventory system is essential for anyone managing a collection, whether it consists of books, art, collectibles, or even everyday household items. A systematic approach not only enhances accessibility but also protects the value and integrity of the collection. As you embark on this journey of organization, you will discover that effective cataloging is more than just a chore; it can be an invigorating process that connects you with your possessions on a deeper level.

The first step in creating a robust cataloging system is to determine the scope of your inventory. Consider the items you want to include and the purpose of your catalog. Are you documenting a collection for insurance purposes, or are you simply seeking to declutter and keep track of your belongings? Understanding your goals will guide your decisions throughout the process. For instance, if you are cataloging a collection of rare books, you might prioritize details such as author, publication date, condition, and any unique features like signatures or annotations.

Once you have established the scope, it's time to decide on the method of cataloging. There are numerous approaches available, ranging from traditional pen-and-paper methods to sophisticated digital systems. For those who enjoy the tactile experience, a journal can serve as a personal log. Each item can be documented with handwritten notes, providing a unique touch that reflects your personality. However, this method may become cumbersome as the collection grows.

Digital cataloging offers advantages in efficiency and organization. Spreadsheet software, such as Microsoft Excel or Google Sheets, enables you to create customizable templates that can easily be sorted and filtered. A digital approach allows for quick updates, making it simpler to add new items or modify existing entries. Various cataloging software applications are also available, designed specifically for collectors. These programs often come with features such as barcode scanning, photo uploads, and reporting tools that can streamline the inventory process.

Whichever method you choose, consistency is crucial. Establish a standard format for entering information.

This could include fields for item name, description, condition, location, acquisition date, and value. Consistency not only facilitates easier searching but also enhances the overall professionalism of your catalog. You might even find joy in creating a unique coding system that reflects your style, like using abbreviations or color coding for different categories of items.

As you begin documenting your collection, take the time to evaluate each item carefully. This is an opportunity to reconnect with your belongings, to appreciate their value and the stories they hold. For instance, a vintage camera might evoke memories of family vacations, while a piece of art could remind you of a cherished friend. Noting down these personal anecdotes adds a layer of emotional significance to your catalog, transforming it from a mere list into a narrative that encapsulates your history.

Photographing each item is a valuable practice that complements your descriptions. Visual records provide a quick reference and can help in identifying items later on. High-quality images, taken from multiple angles, can be particularly useful for insurance documentation or when considering the sale of collectibles. Beyond practicality, photographs can also inspire creativity, encouraging you to explore new ways to display or interact with the items.

Once the cataloging process is underway, think about organization. Group similar items together to create a logical flow within your inventory. Whether you prefer categorization by type, size, color, or value, find a system that works for you. An art collection, for instance, could be organized by artist, medium, or genre, while a library might be sorted by author, title, or subject matter. This thoughtful arrangement not only enhances usability but also brings a sense of harmony to your collection.

In addition to organizing your inventory, consider the physical storage of your items. The environment in which your collection is kept greatly impacts its longevity. Different items may require unique conditions; for example, art pieces may need to be stored in climate-controlled environments, while books benefit from being kept away from direct sunlight. Invest in suitable storage solutions, such as archival boxes for documents or display cases for collectibles, ensuring that your possessions are well protected.

Regular maintenance of your catalog is just as important as the initial setup. Schedule periodic reviews to keep your inventory up to date. This practice not only helps in tracking new acquisitions and disposals but also allows you to reassess the condition of your items. Perhaps a beloved piece of furniture has shown wear over time, or a cherished book has become damaged. Documenting these changes ensures that your catalog remains an accurate reflection of your collection.

Digital catalogs offer additional features that can enhance your inventory management. Many applications allow for cloud storage, enabling you to access your catalog from anywhere. This is particularly advantageous for those who attend flea markets, estate sales, or auctions, as you can reference your catalog in real-time, preventing duplicate purchases or regrettable sales. Furthermore, some software packages include features for tracking valuations, helping you to understand the current market worth of your items.

Engaging with fellow collectors can enrich your cataloging experience. Joining online forums, social media groups, or local clubs can provide insights and tips on managing collections. Sharing your cataloging methods and learning from others may introduce you to new strategies and tools that enhance your own practices. Additionally, these communities often serve as valuable resources for appraisals, allowing you to gauge the value of your items through collective knowledge.

Ultimately, cataloging and inventory management is an ongoing journey, not a destination. The process invites reflection on your possessions, encourages organization, and fosters a deeper appreciation for the things you own. As you navigate the intricacies of your collection, you may discover that each item has its own story to tell, connecting you to your past while paving the way for future endeavors. By committing to a thoughtful cataloging system, you not only safeguard your treasures but also create a rich tapestry of memories and experiences that will last a lifetime.

Protecting Your Collection

The satisfaction of building a collection, whether it consists of antiques, rare books, art, or any other cherished items, is often accompanied by the responsibility of protecting those treasures. Each piece holds not just monetary value but also sentimental significance, making it crucial to safeguard them from potential threats such as environmental damage, theft, or even neglect. The journey of protecting a collection requires thoughtful consideration and proactive measures, ensuring that your valued possessions remain intact for years to come.

One of the primary threats to any collection is environmental factors. Temperature fluctuations, humidity levels, and exposure to light can all contribute to the deterioration of items over time. For instance, paper-based materials such as books and documents thrive in a stable environment with controlled temperatures, ideally around 65-70°F (18-21°C) with a relative humidity of 40-50%. Anything outside of this range can lead to warping, fading, or mold growth. Similarly, artworks on paper or canvas can suffer from light exposure, causing colors to fade and degrading the materials. Investing in climate control systems and using UV-filtering glass for display frames can greatly mitigate these risks.

Another essential aspect of protecting your collection is proper storage. The way items are stored can significantly affect their longevity. For books, consider using shelves that allow for vertical storage without overcrowding. Avoid placing them in direct sunlight or near heat sources like radiators. Archival boxes, acid-free folders, and protective sleeves can provide an extra layer of security for more delicate items. When it comes to collectibles, such as stamps or coins, specialized albums and holders designed for preservation can help maintain their condition. It's worth remembering that sometimes less is more; overstuffed storage spaces can lead to damage from pressure and friction.

Physical security is also a critical consideration, especially for valuable items. The possibility of theft or damage should never be underestimated. Basic measures like installing a robust locking system on display cabinets or securing items in a dedicated room can deter casual theft. For those with particularly valuable collections, investing in a security system with surveillance cameras and alarms can provide peace of mind. Additionally, keeping an updated inventory with photographs and detailed descriptions of each item will not only help in case of theft but also aid in insurance assessments.

Insurance is an often-overlooked component of protecting a collection. It is vital to have a comprehensive policy that covers loss, theft, or damage to your items. Many collectors make the mistake of assuming their homeowner's insurance will suffice. Specialized insurance for collectibles can provide coverage tailored to the unique needs of your collection, often at a reasonable cost. Documenting the value of your items through appraisals can also be beneficial, giving you a clearer picture of what needs coverage and ensuring that you are adequately compensated in the event of loss.

In addition to physical and environmental protection, regular maintenance and inspection are crucial. Taking the time to periodically assess the condition of your items allows you to catch potential problems early. For instance, inspecting books for signs of pests, such as silverfish or booklice, can prevent infestations that could wreak havoc on your collection. Similarly, artworks should be examined for any signs of deterioration, such as cracking or flaking paint. Establishing a routine maintenance schedule helps ensure that your collection remains in optimal condition.

When handling items from your collection, it's essential to practice good preservation techniques. Always wash your hands before touching delicate materials to avoid transferring oils or dirt. Use gloves when handling photographs or documents, as the natural oils from your skin can cause irreversible damage. For more substantial items, such as sculptures or ceramics, ensure that your hands are clean and dry, and support the item properly to prevent accidental drops or damage.

Education plays a vital role in protecting your collection. The more you know about the materials, history, and best preservation practices related to your items, the better equipped you will be to care for them. Books, online resources, and workshops can provide valuable information specific to your collection type. Networking with fellow collectors can also yield insights and tips that may not be readily available in print. Sharing knowledge and experiences can lead to a more profound understanding of how to protect and enjoy your collection.

As your collection grows, consider seeking the assistance of professionals. Conservators and restorers possess specialized skills that can help maintain or restore items that have suffered wear or damage. Their expertise can be invaluable, especially for unique or irreplaceable pieces. When engaging with professionals, always ensure they are reputable and experienced in the specific type of item you need assistance with. It's worth investing in quality care for your most treasured possessions.

Finally, embrace the idea of sharing your collection with others. By creating a display that is open to friends and family, you not only celebrate your passion but also foster a community that appreciates the same interests. This invitation to share can also act as a form of protection; when items are seen and appreciated, it is less likely they will be neglected or forgotten. Hosting events or joining local collecting groups can create opportunities for connection, education, and collective responsibility for preserving the items you all cherish.

Protecting a collection is an ongoing commitment, one that involves a careful balance of knowledge, resources, and proactive measures. By understanding the unique needs of your items, investing in proper care and security, and educating yourself about preservation techniques, you can ensure that your collection remains a source of joy and pride for years to come. Ultimately, safeguarding your collection is about honoring the stories, memories, and histories that each piece represents, allowing future generations to appreciate and connect with them as you do.

Storage Solutions for Small Collectibles

Finding the right storage solutions for small collectibles can be as rewarding as the hunt for the items themselves. Each piece in a collection, whether it's a rare coin, a delicate figurine, or a vintage toy, carries its own story and significance. Proper storage not only preserves these treasures but also enhances your enjoyment of them. When done thoughtfully, storage can elevate the presentation of your collectibles while ensuring their safety and longevity.

The first consideration in selecting storage solutions is the type of collectible you have. Each category has its own unique requirements. For instance, a collection of stamps demands different care than a set of small porcelain figurines. Stamps should be stored in acid-free albums or protective sleeves to prevent damage from light, moisture, and physical wear. Meanwhile, porcelain items require cushioned storage, ideally in boxes lined with soft materials to avoid chipping or breaking. Understanding the specific needs of your collectibles will guide you in choosing appropriate storage options.

When it comes to small collectibles, display cases can serve dual purposes: protection and presentation. A well-designed display case not only showcases your items but also keeps them safe from dust, light, and handling. Glass-fronted cabinets are particularly effective, as they provide visibility while acting as a barrier against environmental factors. Consider the aesthetics of your display case; a vintage-style cabinet may complement your collection of antiques, while a sleek, modern display can enhance contemporary items. The right case can become a part of your decor, turning your collection into a conversational centerpiece.

For those whose collectibles are susceptible to fading or deterioration, climate control is essential. Fluctuations in temperature and humidity can wreak havoc on sensitive materials. Items like coins and paper products benefit from being stored in a climate-controlled environment, ideally between 50-70% relative humidity. Use silica gel packets in storage boxes to absorb excess moisture, and ensure that the space is free from direct sunlight. Basements and attics may seem like convenient storage areas, but they can often have unpredictable temperature and humidity levels. Investing in proper storage space is a small price to pay for the protection of your cherished items.

If your collection is extensive, consider organizing it into categories to make access easier. Grouping similar items together reduces clutter and helps you locate pieces quickly. For example, if you collect small action figures, you might categorize them by series, character, or manufacturer. Clear plastic bins can be a practical solution for this type of organization, allowing you to see the contents at a glance while keeping them protected. Labeling each bin or box will further enhance accessibility, making it simple to find what you need without unnecessary rummaging.

For those who appreciate the tactile experience of their collectibles, a dedicated display shelf can offer a delightful solution. Floating shelves provide a minimalist way to showcase items while keeping them within reach. Arrange your collectibles in a way that creates visual interest; consider varying heights and sizes to create a dynamic display. Using small risers or stands can help add dimension and draw attention to standout pieces. However, it's crucial to ensure that the shelves are securely mounted and that heavier items are placed on lower shelves to prevent accidents.

When considering storage for small collectibles, materials matter. Avoid using cardboard boxes that can deteriorate over time, releasing acids that may damage your items. Instead, opt for acid-free plastic bins or archival-quality boxes. These materials are designed to protect collectibles from environmental harm while providing a sturdy structure for storage. For items that require additional cushioning, such as fragile ceramics or glass, consider using bubble wrap or foam inserts to prevent movement during storage.

Another important aspect of storing small collectibles is the need for regular maintenance. Just as you would routinely check your car or home appliances, make it a habit to assess the condition of your collection periodically. Dust accumulation can be more damaging than one might think, particularly for delicate items. Regularly dusting your collectibles with a soft cloth will help maintain their appearance and prevent any build-up that could lead to deterioration. For items that are particularly valuable or fragile, consider professional cleaning services that specialize in preserving collectibles.

As your collection grows, the need for more storage solutions may arise. This is a perfect opportunity to evaluate your collection and determine if there are items that no longer hold the same significance. Sometimes, letting go of certain pieces can create space for new acquisitions and allow you to focus on the items that truly resonate with you. In the world of collecting, quality often outweighs quantity. By curating your collection, you can create a more meaningful and manageable inventory.

Participating in local collector clubs or online communities can also provide valuable insights into storage solutions. Fellow collectors often share their experiences and recommendations, offering tips that you may not have considered. Networking can lead to friendships and collaborations, fostering a sense of community around your shared interests. Additionally, attending workshops or seminars can provide professional guidance on the best practices for storing collectibles.

Lastly, consider the option of digital inventory management. Keeping a digital catalog of your collection allows you to track items, including their condition and location, with ease. High-quality photographs paired with detailed descriptions can help you remember the stories behind each piece. This practice is particularly beneficial if you decide to insure your collection, as it provides documentation of its value and condition. Digital tools can help streamline the organization process, making it easier to manage your collection as it continues to evolve.

Creating effective storage solutions for small collectibles is a journey that combines practicality with creativity. By understanding the unique needs of your items, investing in proper storage materials, and maintaining regular care, you can ensure that your collection remains a source of joy and pride. Each piece you store tells a story, and with the right approach to protection and organization, those stories can be cherished for generations to come. Embrace the process, and watch as your collection flourishes in a well-preserved sanctuary.

Sharing Your Collection with Others

The joy of collecting often finds its true expression when shared with others. Each item in your collection carries a story, a memory, or a piece of history waiting to be unveiled. Inviting friends, family, and fellow enthusiasts into your world of collectibles not only enhances your appreciation for your items but also fosters connections that can enrich your collecting journey. Sharing your collection can take many forms, from informal gatherings to organized exhibitions, each providing unique opportunities for engagement and conversation.

One of the simplest ways to share your collection is through hosting a gathering at your home. Imagine inviting a few close friends over for an afternoon of coffee and conversation, with your cherished items displayed for all to see. This intimate setting encourages dialogue, allowing you to share the stories behind your pieces. Perhaps a vintage record player sits on a shelf, accompanied by a collection of vinyl records. Sharing how you stumbled upon it at a flea market can spark interest, prompting friends to recount their own stories or memories related to music. These shared experiences create a sense of camaraderie and can deepen relationships.

Consider creating a thematic display for your gathering. Whether it's a showcase of items from a particular era, a collection of art from local artists, or a group of rare books, a cohesive theme can enhance the aesthetic appeal and spark curiosity. You might even incorporate games or trivia related to your collection, turning the event into a fun and interactive experience. Sharing knowledge in this manner not only entertains but also educates your guests, transforming them into fellow enthusiasts.

Social media platforms offer another avenue for sharing your collection with a broader audience. Posting pictures and stories about your items can engage friends and followers who may not have the opportunity to see your collection in person. Use hashtags related to your collection type to connect with like-minded individuals and join communities that share your passion. These online platforms can serve as a source of inspiration, as you discover new ideas for displaying or caring for your collectibles. Interaction with other collectors can lead to fruitful exchanges, where tips, advice, and even trade opportunities flourish.

For those looking to take their sharing a step further, consider organizing an exhibition. This could be a solo exhibit in your local community center or a collaborative effort with other collectors. Displaying your collection publicly not only showcases your passion but also raises awareness about collecting as a hobby. Visitors will be intrigued to learn about the history and significance of each piece, and the experience can inspire others to start their own collections. Collaborating with local galleries or museums can enhance the legitimacy of your exhibition and attract a wider audience.

Participating in collector fairs or conventions is another exciting way to share your collection. These events often draw enthusiasts from various backgrounds and interests, creating a bustling atmosphere filled with energy and excitement. Setting up a booth or table allows you to display your items and engage with fellow collectors, sharing insights and stories while learning from others. These events are also excellent opportunities for networking, whether you're looking to buy, sell, or simply connect with other enthusiasts.

If you have a particularly impressive collection, consider contributing to a local library or educational institution. Many libraries host exhibitions that highlight community interests, and displaying your items can benefit both you and the institution. Visitors gain access to unique pieces of history, while you have the chance to share your knowledge and passion in a more formal setting. Collaborating with educators can also lead to workshops or lectures where you can teach others about the nuances of your collection.

As you engage with others about your collection, remember the importance of storytelling. Each item has its own narrative, and weaving these tales into conversations can captivate your audience. Share the journey of how you acquired each piece, the research you've done, and the connections you've made along the way. Your enthusiasm will be contagious, and others may find themselves inspired to delve into the world of collecting or to appreciate the stories behind their possessions.

When sharing your collection, be mindful of the emotional connections that others may have with similar items. Everyone has their own story, and by creating an open environment for discussion, you allow those around you to share their experiences. Perhaps a friend recognizes a toy from their childhood in your collection, igniting a flood of memories. Encouraging these exchanges fosters a sense of belonging and helps build a community of collectors who support and inspire one another.

Documentation plays a vital role in sharing your collection. Keeping an organized record of your items, complete with photographs and descriptions, can enhance the experience for yourself and your audience. This archive not only serves as a reference for potential buyers or fellow collectors but also preserves the history of your collection. Consider creating a digital catalog that can easily be shared online, allowing others to explore your collection from anywhere.

As you share your collection, be prepared for questions and discussions. Engaging with curious minds can lead to meaningful conversations and new friendships. You may find that someone has a wealth of knowledge about a particular item or a connection to a similar collectible. Embrace these interactions, as they can provide fresh perspectives and insights into your collection, enriching your understanding and appreciation for each piece.

Ultimately, sharing your collection is a celebration of passion, memory, and community. Whether it's through personal gatherings, social media posts, exhibitions, or collector fairs, the act of sharing transforms solitary enjoyment into a collective experience. The stories entwined with each item take on new life as they are shared with others, creating a tapestry of connections that can last a lifetime. Open your doors, invite others in, and watch as your love for collecting flourishes in a vibrant community of fellow enthusiasts.

Chapter 5: The Community of Collectors

Finding Fellow Collectors

The thrill of collecting often expands exponentially when shared with others who share the same passion. Finding fellow collectors can elevate your experience, allowing you to exchange knowledge, trade items, and forge friendships that enrich your collecting journey. Whether you are a seasoned collector or just starting, connecting with others in the community offers numerous rewards and opportunities for growth.

One of the most effective ways to find fellow collectors is to tap into local clubs and organizations dedicated to specific types of collectibles. Many cities have groups that meet regularly, providing a platform for enthusiasts to gather and share their interests. These clubs often host events, such as swap meets or educational seminars, which can be excellent opportunities for networking. Attending a meeting can feel like stepping into a treasure trove of shared enthusiasm, where every conversation can lead to insights or potential trades. Even if you don't find an immediate connection, being part of such a community can help you stay informed about upcoming events and meet fellow collectors.

Online platforms have revolutionized the way collectors connect. Social media groups, forums, and specialized websites cater to nearly every collecting niche imaginable. Joining these digital communities allows you to interact with people from all over the world, expanding your network beyond geographical limitations. Facebook groups, for instance, often serve as vibrant hubs for discussion, showcasing items for sale, sharing tips, or discussing the latest trends in the collecting world. Reddit also hosts numerous subreddits dedicated to specific types of collectibles, where you can engage in conversations and learn from the experiences of others.

Attending collector fairs and conventions is another thrilling avenue for meeting like-minded individuals. These events bring together enthusiasts, dealers, and collectors under one roof, creating an energetic atmosphere filled with the excitement of discovery. As you stroll through the aisles, the sounds of lively conversations and the sight of countless treasures can be invigorating. Strike up conversations with fellow attendees; you'll find that many are eager to share their knowledge and stories. Exchanging contact information can lead to new friendships that extend beyond the event, allowing you to keep in touch and collaborate on future endeavors.

Networking at these events can also reveal opportunities for mentorship. Experienced collectors often take newcomers under their wing, offering guidance and sharing valuable insights about the intricacies of the hobby. Don't hesitate to approach someone whose collection you admire; a simple compliment can open the door to deeper conversations. Many collectors are passionate about teaching others, and you might find yourself learning about preservation techniques, valuation methods, or even the history of your specific items.

Local libraries and community centers may host workshops or lectures on collecting topics, providing another avenue to meet fellow enthusiasts. These events often attract individuals who are eager to learn, and the collaborative environment fosters connections. Participating in workshops not only enhances your knowledge but also allows you to engage with others who share your interests. Discussing what you learn with new acquaintances can lead to friendships grounded in a shared commitment to collecting.

Consider reaching out to local antique shops, galleries, or specialty stores. Many of these establishments have bulletin boards where collectors can post notices about upcoming events or groups. Building relationships with shop owners can also provide insights into local collecting communities. They often know who the key players are in your area and can connect you with other collectors. Moreover, frequent visits to these shops can lead to serendipitous encounters with fellow enthusiasts, sparking conversations that may lead to long-lasting friendships.

Participating in online auctions and marketplaces can also help you meet other collectors. Engaging with sellers and buyers not only enhances your knowledge of pricing and trends but also opens avenues for conversation. Many collectors frequent these platforms, and you may find individuals who are eager to discuss their collections or share collecting tips. Building rapport with these individuals can lead to fruitful exchanges and potential collaborations.

Another effective strategy for finding fellow collectors is to start your own blog or YouTube channel. Sharing your collecting journey and insights can attract individuals with similar interests. By documenting your experiences, you create a platform for interaction, inviting others to comment and share their own stories. The collecting community thrives on shared experiences, and your content can foster connections with fellow enthusiasts who resonate with your perspective.

Joining national or international collector associations can provide even broader access to fellow collectors. Many of these organizations host events, publish newsletters, and offer resources that can enhance your collecting experience. Membership often includes access to exclusive events, educational materials, and forums where you can engage with collectors from diverse backgrounds. These associations are particularly valuable if you are focused on a specific type of collectible, such as coins, stamps, or vintage toys.

As you navigate the path of finding fellow collectors, remember the importance of being open and approachable. Attend events with a mindset of curiosity and a willingness to engage. Ask questions, share your experiences, and listen actively to others. The more you invest in building connections, the richer your collecting experience will become. Authentic connections can lead to collaborations, trades, and friendships that last a lifetime.

Building a network of fellow collectors can also lead to opportunities for group excursions or field trips.

Organizing a visit to a museum, an auction house, or a notable collection can foster camaraderie and create shared memories. These outings provide a chance to bond over common interests while exploring new realms of collecting. Plus, experiencing the excitement of discovery together can deepen your connections with fellow enthusiasts.

Ultimately, the journey of finding fellow collectors is as rewarding as the pursuit of the items themselves. Each connection can offer fresh perspectives, insights, and friendships that enrich your collecting experience. Sharing knowledge, stories, and passion creates a vibrant community, where the thrill of discovery is multiplied. Embrace the opportunities that come your way, and allow your love for collecting to lead you to the remarkable individuals who share your journey.

The Role of Online Forums and Social Media

The landscape of collecting has evolved dramatically with the advent of online forums and social media, transforming how enthusiasts connect, share, and grow their collections. These digital platforms have become essential tools for collectors, offering a space to exchange knowledge, seek advice, and build communities that transcend geographical boundaries.

Online forums dedicated to specific types of collectibles are an invaluable resource. These platforms allow collectors to dive deep into niche interests, from vintage toys and rare stamps to antique coins and comic books. The structure of these forums encourages discussion, enabling members to post questions, share photos, and engage in lively debates about the value and history of their items. For example, a collector may post a photo of a newly acquired piece, inviting feedback on its authenticity or estimated value. Responses can range from seasoned experts offering detailed insights to fellow collectors sharing similar experiences, creating a rich tapestry of knowledge that benefits everyone involved.

One of the most appealing aspects of these forums is the sense of community they foster. Many collectors find a kindred spirit among their peers, people who understand the thrill of the hunt and the joy of discovery. These connections often extend beyond the screen, leading to friendships that can last a lifetime. Engaging in discussions about personal collections can spark meaningful relationships, as individuals share not just their items but also the stories behind them. Imagine a collector recounting how they stumbled upon a rare find at a flea market, only to discover that another forum member had a similar experience years ago. These shared stories help build camaraderie and deepen the appreciation for the hobby.

Social media platforms have further enhanced the experience of collecting. Sites like Instagram and Facebook allow collectors to showcase their items visually, reaching a wider audience and attracting interest from individuals who may never have crossed paths otherwise. Posting photos of your collection can be both a personal archive and a way to inspire others. The hashtags associated with posts can help connect like-minded individuals, creating a web of shared interests that can lead to new friendships and collaborations.

Instagram, in particular, thrives on visuals, making it a perfect platform for collectors. Users can curate their feeds, showcasing items in aesthetically pleasing ways. A collector of vintage vinyl records might create a beautiful display of album covers, complete with background stories about each artist or track. This not only shares the beauty of the collection but also educates followers about the music's historical context. The comments section often becomes a lively discussion, where followers share their own experiences or express interest in particular albums.

Facebook groups dedicated to collecting provide a more interactive experience. These groups often have thousands of members, allowing for a vibrant exchange of ideas and items. Members can post their latest finds, ask for advice on preservation techniques, or seek recommendations for reputable dealers. The diverse backgrounds of group members enrich discussions, offering a broad range of perspectives that can enhance one's understanding of the collecting landscape. Additionally, many groups facilitate buying and selling among members, providing a trusted environment to make transactions.

The networking potential of social media cannot be overstated. Many collectors have successfully expanded their collections through connections made online. A casual interaction in a forum might lead to a private sale, a trade, or even an invitation to an exclusive collector event. These opportunities can open doors to new items that may not be available through conventional channels. Imagine a collector who, after posting a photo of a rare action figure, receives a direct message from another collector who has the missing piece. This kind of interaction illustrates how social media can foster a sense of collaboration and mutual benefit among collectors.

Moreover, online platforms serve as excellent educational resources. Collectors can find instructional videos, articles, and expert opinions with just a few clicks. YouTube, for instance, is filled with channels dedicated to specific collectibles, offering tutorials on everything from cleaning and preserving items to tips on spotting fakes. Engaging with these resources can enhance your collecting skills and deepen your knowledge, making you a more informed and confident collector.

Another significant advantage of online forums and social media is the ability to stay updated on trends and market fluctuations. Collectors can quickly learn about rising values, new releases, and upcoming events. This real-time access to information helps collectors make informed decisions about their purchases and sales. Being part of a community means you're not just reacting to changes; you're actively participating in discussions that shape the market landscape.

However, navigating these platforms requires a level of discernment. With the vast amount of information available, it's essential to critically evaluate sources and advice. While many members are genuine enthusiasts looking to share their knowledge, others may not have the expertise they claim. Engaging in discussions and asking questions can help you filter out trustworthy information from less reliable sources. Building a reputation within these communities often comes from consistent, respectful participation and sharing your own knowledge as you learn.

Privacy and safety are also important considerations when interacting online. Sharing personal information can expose you to risks, so it's wise to be cautious. When buying or selling items, ensure that the platforms you use provide a degree of security and trust. Many collectors have found success in making transactions through established platforms that offer buyer and seller protections, reducing the risk of fraud.

As you immerse yourself in the world of online forums and social media, remember that the journey of collecting is as much about the connections you make as it is about the items you acquire. Engaging with fellow enthusiasts can lead to a deeper appreciation of your collection and the stories behind each piece. The friendships you forge, the knowledge you gain, and the inspiration you receive can transform your collecting experience into something truly extraordinary. Embrace the digital age of collecting, and allow these platforms to enrich your journey, connecting you with a vibrant community of like-minded individuals who share your passion.

Attending Collectible Shows and Expos

Attending collectible shows and expos is an exhilarating experience for any enthusiast. These events provide a unique opportunity to immerse oneself in the world of collecting, where passion and excitement fill the air. The atmosphere buzzes with energy as collectors, dealers, and curious newcomers gather under one roof, all drawn by a shared love for unique and rare items. Whether you're a seasoned collector or just beginning your journey, these events can significantly enhance your appreciation for your chosen collectibles.

Walking through the aisles of a collectible show is akin to stepping into a treasure hunt. Rows upon rows of tables and booths showcase a diverse array of items, each with its own story and history. The sight of vintage toys, rare coins, vintage comic books, or unique art pieces can be overwhelming in the best possible way. As you navigate through the displays, you might find yourself captivated by an item that sparks a memory or a sense of nostalgia, prompting you to learn more about its background. The tactile nature of these events allows you to examine each piece closely, inspecting its details and understanding its significance.

One of the most valuable aspects of attending these shows is the opportunity to interact directly with dealers and fellow collectors. Engaging in conversation can provide insights that you might not find through online research. Dealers often possess extensive knowledge about their products, including how they were sourced and the stories behind them. Ask questions, share your interests, and don't hesitate to seek advice. Many dealers are passionate about their items and enjoy educating others about their significance, making them excellent resources for information.

Networking is another powerful benefit of attending collectible shows. These events attract a diverse crowd, from novice collectors to seasoned experts. Striking up conversations with fellow attendees can lead to new friendships and connections within the collecting community. You might meet someone who shares your specific interest or has insights into the latest trends in the market. Exchanging contact information can pave the way for future discussions, trades, or even collaborative ventures. A casual conversation over a rare find can blossom into a meaningful relationship that enriches your collecting journey.

For many collectors, the thrill of the hunt is a key motivation. Shows and expos provide a unique environment where you can discover items that may not be available anywhere else. Dealers often bring their best pieces, including rare and hard-to-find collectibles, specifically for these events. This creates an exciting atmosphere of competition among buyers, as everyone seeks to find the next gem. The adrenaline rush of spotting a coveted item can lead to spontaneous purchases and trades that you might not have considered otherwise.

It's also essential to come prepared when attending these shows. Having a clear idea of what you're looking for can help you focus your efforts. Create a list of specific items or types of collectibles you hope to find, along with any details about their value or rarity. Researching beforehand can equip you with the knowledge needed to identify good deals or potential fakes. While spontaneity is part of the fun, being informed can help ensure you make wise purchasing decisions.

Budgeting is another vital aspect to consider. The excitement of being surrounded by so many collectibles can lead to impulse buys, so it's wise to set a spending limit before you arrive. This not only helps you manage your finances but also encourages you to think critically about each potential purchase. Prioritize the items on your list, and if you come across something unexpected that truly speaks to you, assess whether it fits within your budget.

When attending shows, consider bringing along tools to assist you in your collecting endeavors. A handheld magnifying glass can help you inspect items for authenticity, while a notepad or app can be useful for recording details about pieces you're interested in. If you're looking to trade or sell, having business cards can facilitate connections with other collectors. You never know when an opportunity might arise to discuss a potential trade or sale.

While the focus of these events is often on buying and selling, they also provide a rich educational experience. Many expos feature workshops, panels, or discussions led by industry experts. Attending these sessions can enhance your understanding of various aspects of collecting, from valuation and preservation techniques to market trends and historical context. Learning from seasoned professionals can help you make more informed decisions and deepen your appreciation for your collectibles.

Experiencing the atmosphere of a collectible show is another integral part of the journey. The excitement and enthusiasm of fellow attendees create an infectious energy that can inspire you. Sharing stories, learning from one another, and reveling in the joy of collecting can transform a simple visit into a memorable event. You might find yourself caught up in conversations about the history of a particular item or the thrill of finding a long-sought piece, reinforcing the sense of community that defines the collecting world.

As the day comes to a close, take a moment to reflect on your experience. What did you learn? Did you make any meaningful connections? Did you find any items that you never expected to discover? These reflections can help you appreciate the value of attending collectible shows beyond just the transactions. It's about the connections, the education, and the shared passion that unites collectors.

Ultimately, attending collectible shows and expos is more than just a shopping trip; it's an immersive journey into a world filled with stories, history, and community. The experience can deepen your understanding of your collection, enhance your passion, and lead to lasting relationships that will enrich your collecting journey. Each show is an opportunity to learn, connect, and discover, making it an essential part of any collector's adventure. Embrace the excitement, engage with fellow enthusiasts, and let the world of collectibles inspire you in ways you never imagined.

Collaborating on Projects

The essence of collaboration often transforms the solitary pursuit of collecting into a dynamic and enriching experience. Working together on projects not only enhances individual skills but also fosters relationships that can lead to lifelong friendships. When collectors unite, they bring diverse perspectives, resources, and expertise to the table, creating a synergy that can elevate their shared endeavors beyond what any single person could achieve alone.

Imagine two collectors with a shared interest in vintage comic books. One has an extensive collection but lacks the technical skills to create an engaging online platform. The other possesses digital marketing expertise but has only a modest collection. Together, they can create a website or social media presence that not only showcases their collections but also serves as a hub for other enthusiasts. By pooling their knowledge and skills, they can reach a wider audience, provide valuable content, and build a community around their shared passion.

Collaborative projects can take on various forms. They can be as simple as co-hosting a local event or as complex as launching a publication dedicated to a specific niche within the collecting world. For instance, a group of collectors passionate about vintage toys might decide to organize a local toy fair. By working together, they can secure a venue, promote the event, and attract vendors and attendees. This not only enhances their visibility within the community but also strengthens bonds among participants. The excitement of bringing people together for a common purpose can be incredibly rewarding, creating memories that last long after the event concludes.

The internet has opened new avenues for collaboration, allowing collectors from different parts of the world to connect and work on projects that may have once seemed impossible. Online forums and social media groups enable like-minded individuals to come together, share ideas, and brainstorm initiatives. Consider the example of a group of collectors who decide to create a documentary exploring the history of a particular collectible. They can divide responsibilities based on individual strengths—some can handle research, others can conduct interviews, and a few can manage video editing. By leveraging each member's expertise, they can produce a compelling narrative that not only celebrates their passion but also educates others about the significance of their hobby.

Collaboration can also lead to innovative projects that would be difficult to undertake individually. For example, a group of coin collectors might collaborate to create a database cataloging rare coins, complete with images, historical context, and valuation data. Each member can contribute their knowledge and resources, ensuring that the database becomes a comprehensive guide for both novice and experienced collectors. This project not only serves the community but also positions the collaborators as thought leaders in their niche.

As you embark on collaborative projects, establishing clear communication is crucial. Open dialogue fosters trust, encourages idea-sharing, and ensures everyone is on the same page. Regular meetings, either in person or virtually, provide an opportunity to discuss progress, address challenges, and celebrate achievements. Utilizing collaborative tools such as shared documents or project management software can streamline the process, making it easier to track contributions and deadlines. Ensuring that everyone feels heard and valued in discussions will enhance the overall experience and strengthen relationships.

Setting shared goals is another essential aspect of successful collaboration. Each member should have a clear understanding of what the project aims to achieve and how their contributions fit into the larger picture. For instance, if a group is working on a collecting guide, defining the target audience and specific topics to cover can help maintain focus and direction. By establishing measurable goals, the team can assess progress and adjust their strategies as needed. Celebrating milestones, no matter how small, will help maintain motivation and enthusiasm throughout the project.

It's important to recognize that challenges may arise during collaborative efforts. Differences in opinions, work styles, or schedules can lead to friction. Approaching these challenges with empathy and a willingness to compromise is vital. Embracing diverse perspectives can lead to innovative solutions and strengthen the collaborative spirit. When conflicts arise, addressing them promptly and respectfully can prevent misunderstandings from escalating and ensure the project remains on track.

Feedback plays a critical role in the collaborative process. Constructive criticism can help refine ideas and improve outcomes. Encouraging an environment where team members feel comfortable sharing their thoughts fosters growth and enhances the quality of the final product. When feedback is delivered thoughtfully, it can inspire creativity and lead to breakthroughs that elevate the project beyond initial expectations.

Celebrating the completion of a collaborative project is an opportunity to reflect on what has been achieved together. Whether it's a successful event, a published guide, or an online platform, taking the time to acknowledge everyone's contributions fosters a sense of accomplishment and strengthens bonds within the group. Sharing the final product with the broader community can also amplify its impact, showcasing the collective effort and expertise that went into creating it.

The experience of collaborating on projects can profoundly impact personal growth as well. Working alongside others challenges you to step outside your comfort zone, enhancing skills you may not have developed otherwise. It encourages adaptability and resilience, as you learn to navigate the dynamics of teamwork. The friendships forged through these collaborative efforts often extend beyond the project itself, enriching your collecting journey in ways you may not have anticipated.

As you delve into the world of collaboration, remember that the process is just as valuable as the outcome. The connections you make, the lessons you learn, and the joy of creating something together can be immensely fulfilling. Embrace the opportunity to work with others, and allow their insights to inspire you. In the realm of collecting, collaboration can open doors to new experiences and possibilities, transforming your passion into a shared adventure that celebrates the unique stories behind every item. Embrace the journey, and let the power of collaboration elevate your collecting experience to new heights.

The Importance of Networking

Networking serves as a cornerstone in the world of collecting, transforming individual pursuits into collective experiences. Through networking, collectors not only expand their knowledge and resources but also cultivate relationships that can profoundly influence their journey. The connections made within this vibrant community can lead to opportunities for collaboration, mentorship, and access to rare items that may not be available through traditional channels.

At its core, networking is about establishing and nurturing relationships. Every collector has a unique story, and sharing those narratives fosters connections that can enrich the experience for everyone involved. When you engage with fellow enthusiasts, whether at a local show or through online forums, you open the door to conversations that can illuminate various aspects of your collecting journey. Talking to someone who has been in the field for decades can provide insights that turn a casual hobby into a passionate pursuit.

The benefits of networking extend beyond mere social interaction. It can be a powerful tool for education. Engaging with others allows you to learn about different collecting strategies, preservation techniques, and market trends. For instance, a seasoned collector might share tips on how to spot counterfeit items, while another might provide guidance on valuing your collection. These conversations can save you time and money, as well as protect you from potential pitfalls. Furthermore, the exchange of knowledge creates a sense of community, reinforcing the idea that collecting is not just an individual endeavor but a shared passion that thrives on collaboration.

Consider the example of a collector who specializes in vintage vinyl records. By attending local meetups and engaging with others online, they may discover a community of enthusiasts who are equally passionate about music history. Through these connections, they could learn about rare pressings or attend exclusive listening parties. Networking can lead to unexpected discoveries, whether it's finding a rare album or learning about historical trends that impact the value of certain records. Such insights can enhance not only the collector's understanding but also their appreciation for the art form itself.

Another significant advantage of networking is the potential for mentorship. Many experienced collectors are eager to share their knowledge with newcomers. Finding a mentor can be invaluable, as it provides guidance and encouragement during the formative stages of your collecting journey. A mentor can help you navigate the complexities of the market, suggest reputable dealers, and even accompany you to shows, providing insights as you explore. This relationship can serve as a source of inspiration, motivating you to delve deeper into your interests and refine your collecting skills.

Networking also opens doors to collaboration. When collectors come together, they can undertake projects that would be difficult to achieve individually. For example, a group of collectors interested in a specific genre might decide to create a joint exhibition or publication that showcases their collections. By pooling resources and expertise, they can present a more comprehensive view of their niche, attracting attention from both the media and potential new collectors. The camaraderie that develops through these collaborative efforts can lead to lasting friendships and a sense of shared accomplishment.

In today's digital age, the avenues for networking have expanded dramatically. Online forums, social media platforms, and specialized websites provide collectors with opportunities to connect across vast distances. Engaging with others through these platforms can be as simple as joining a Facebook group or participating in discussions on a dedicated forum. These interactions allow you to share your experiences, ask questions, and seek advice from a global community of collectors. This virtual networking can be particularly beneficial for those whose interests might not have a local community, offering a sense of belonging that transcends geographic limitations.

However, the impact of networking is not solely confined to the exchange of knowledge and collaboration. It also plays a crucial role in sourcing collectible items. Many collectors find that their best acquisitions come through personal connections rather than traditional retail channels. A fellow collector might offer to sell you a coveted piece from their collection or introduce you to a dealer who specializes in hard-to-find items. This word-of-mouth network can often yield better prices and greater authenticity than purchasing items from unfamiliar sources.

When approaching networking, it's essential to be genuine and respectful. Building relationships takes time, and it's vital to approach interactions with a mindset of curiosity and openness. Instead of focusing solely on what you can gain, consider how you can contribute to the community. Sharing your insights, offering assistance, or simply engaging in meaningful conversations can create a positive impression and establish trust. This reciprocity fosters a supportive environment where everyone benefits from each other's experiences.

Additionally, attending collectible shows and expos can be a great way to expand your network. These events bring together collectors from all walks of life, providing an ideal platform for meeting new people and exchanging ideas. Striking up conversations with vendors, fellow attendees, or speakers can lead to valuable connections. Don't hesitate to introduce yourself and express your interests. The more you engage, the more likely you are to discover new avenues for your collecting journey.

As you continue to build your network, remember that maintaining relationships is just as important as establishing them. Follow up with new acquaintances, whether through social media or email. Share updates about your collection, inquire about theirs, or suggest future meetups. These small gestures can reinforce connections and keep the lines of communication open. Ultimately, the strength of your network will depend on the effort you invest in nurturing those relationships.

Networking is a powerful tool that can significantly enhance your collecting experience. Whether through face-to-face interactions at shows or online discussions in forums, the connections you make will enrich your journey in countless ways. The knowledge, support, and opportunities that arise from these relationships can transform your passion into a thriving community of shared interests and mutual growth. Embrace the power of networking, and watch how it deepens your appreciation for collecting, leading to a more fulfilling and rewarding experience. The world of collecting is vast, and with the right connections, you can navigate it with confidence, enthusiasm, and excitement.

Chapter 6: Stories Behind the Collectibles

Personal Narratives: Why We Collect

Personal narratives are the threads that weave together the diverse tapestry of collecting. Each story is unique, shaped by individual experiences, emotions, and motivations. Understanding why we collect often requires delving into these personal histories, as they reveal the deeper significance behind our pursuits. Whether driven by nostalgia, passion, or the thrill of the hunt, collectors often find that their motivations are as varied as the items they seek.

For many, the journey of collecting begins in childhood. Imagine a young boy who inherits a box of toy cars from his father. Each car is not merely a piece of plastic but a vessel of memories, a tangible connection to family stories shared during lazy afternoons. As he grows older, the boy becomes a man who scours flea markets and online listings, searching for rare models that spark joy and remind him of those cherished moments. The act of collecting becomes a way to honor his past while creating new memories. Nostalgia acts as a powerful motivator, often driving collectors to seek items that resonate with their personal histories.

Nostalgia, however, isn't the only reason people collect. For some, the motivation is rooted in passion and appreciation for a particular subject. Take, for example, a woman with a deep love for vintage fashion. Each piece in her collection tells a story of artistry, craftsmanship, and cultural history. She finds herself captivated by the intricate details of a 1920s flapper dress or the bold patterns of a 1970s maxi dress. Her pursuit is not merely about ownership; it's about preserving the past and celebrating the creativity that has shaped fashion over the decades. This passion fuels her to attend estate sales, auctions, and swap meets, where she can uncover hidden gems that contribute to her ever-growing collection.

Then there are those whose motivations lie in the thrill of the hunt. The excitement of discovering a rare item can evoke a rush akin to a treasure hunt. Picture a collector who spends weekends combing through antique shops and garage sales, eyes scanning the shelves for something extraordinary. Each find becomes a mini-celebration, whether it's an old vinyl record, a unique piece of art, or an obscure comic book. The chase itself can become an addictive pursuit, creating a sense of adventure that makes the hobby exhilarating. The act of searching, bargaining, and finally acquiring that elusive item becomes an integral part of the collecting experience, transforming the collector into a modern-day explorer.

For others, collecting can also serve as a form of self-expression. A collector of mid-century modern furniture may find that each piece reflects not only aesthetic preferences but also personal values. The clean lines and functional designs resonate with a desire for simplicity and elegance in life. This connection to the items in their collection fosters a sense of identity, allowing them to showcase their tastes and values in their living spaces. Each acquisition becomes a statement, a reflection of who they are and what they cherish.

Additionally, collecting can fulfill a human need for connection and community. Think about a collector who joins a local club dedicated to a specific interest, such as stamps or rare coins. Through meetings and events, they form friendships with fellow enthusiasts who share their passion. The camaraderie that develops within these groups creates a supportive network, where members exchange stories, trade items, and celebrate each other's successes. This sense of belonging can be incredibly fulfilling, transforming what might be a solitary pursuit into a shared journey.

Another layer to the narrative of collecting is the historical aspect. Some collectors are motivated by a desire to preserve history and educate others. A historian who collects artifacts from a specific time period may feel a profound responsibility to safeguard these items for future generations. Their passion goes beyond personal enjoyment; it becomes a mission to ensure that the stories behind these artifacts are not lost. This commitment to preservation can drive collectors to share their knowledge through exhibitions, lectures, or community events, fostering a greater appreciation for history among the public.

The act of collecting can also be therapeutic. For some individuals, the process provides a sense of control in a chaotic world. The meticulous organization of a collection can be soothing, allowing the collector to create order from the chaos of everyday life. Delving into the stories behind each item can offer a form of escapism, a way to momentarily step away from stressors and immerse oneself in a world of passion and creativity. This therapeutic aspect can make collecting not just a hobby but a vital source of comfort and joy.

As the narratives unfold, it becomes evident that collecting is often intertwined with our identities. Each acquisition is more than just an item; it embodies a piece of our stories. The collector who proudly displays their extensive collection of sports memorabilia is not merely showcasing items; they are sharing their love for the game, the memories of exhilarating victories, and the bonds formed with family and friends while watching games together.

In the end, the reasons behind our collections are as diverse as the items themselves. Whether driven by nostalgia, passion, adventure, self-expression, community, preservation, or therapy, personal narratives shape our collecting journeys in profound ways. These stories create connections not only to the items we cherish but also to the people we meet along the way. Embracing these narratives enriches the experience, reminding us that collecting is not just about what we gather but also about the memories we create and the relationships we forge. Each collection tells a story, and within those stories lies the heart of what it means to collect. As we reflect on our own motivations and those of others, we appreciate the beauty of this shared journey, where every item holds a tale waiting to be told.

The Stories of Famous Collectors

The world of collecting is rich with stories, particularly those of renowned collectors who have left indelible marks on their fields. These individuals not only amassed impressive collections but also shaped cultural landscapes, inspired generations, and transformed their passions into legacies. Their journeys reveal the profound ways in which collecting can intersect with history, art, and personal identity, offering valuable lessons for anyone who shares a love for the hunt.

Consider the story of J. Paul Getty, the oil magnate whose passion for antiquities led him to create one of the most significant art collections in the world. Getty's journey began in the early 20th century when he started acquiring pieces that spanned centuries and continents. His discerning eye and willingness to invest in lesser-known artists set him apart from his contemporaries. As he traveled through Europe, he sought out not just the well-known masterpieces but also hidden treasures that captivated his imagination. This pursuit culminated in the establishment of the Getty Museum in Los Angeles, which now houses an extensive collection of European paintings, sculptures, and decorative arts. Getty's story exemplifies how a passionate collector can contribute to the preservation and appreciation of art, transforming personal interests into a public legacy that educates and inspires.

Another fascinating figure in the collecting world is Charles E. Hummel, an avid collector of American folk art. Hummel's journey began in the 1950s when he stumbled upon a small, hand-carved wooden figure at a flea market. Captivated by its charm and the story behind its creation, he began to explore the genre more deeply. Over the years, Hummel amassed an impressive collection that included everything from quilts to pottery, each piece telling its own unique narrative. His love for folk art was not merely about ownership; it was about understanding the cultural heritage it represented. Hummel became a vocal advocate for folk art, sharing his knowledge through lectures, exhibitions, and publications. His commitment to educating others on the significance of these ordinary yet extraordinary objects illustrates how personal passion can elevate an entire genre and foster a deeper appreciation for cultural craftsmanship.

Then there's the story of Sir Thomas Phillips, a 19th-century book collector whose obsession with literature led him to acquire one of the largest private libraries of his time. Phillips's passion for books began at a young age, fueled by an insatiable curiosity about the written word. He meticulously sought out rare and valuable editions, often traveling great distances to acquire them. His collection, which included over 60,000 volumes, was not only a testament to his love for literature but also a reflection of his belief in the importance of preserving knowledge. Phillips's library became a resource for scholars and bibliophiles alike, and upon his death, it was sold off in a series of auctions, dispersing his treasures across the globe. His story reminds us that collecting can serve as a bridge between the past and the future, ensuring that knowledge and culture endure beyond our lifetimes.

The narrative of famous collectors is not solely confined to art, literature, and antiquities. The world of sports memorabilia also boasts notable figures, such as the late Keith Olbermann. Known for his career as a sports journalist and commentator, Olbermann's passion for collecting sports cards began in his childhood, when he would trade cards with friends. Over the years, he amassed a remarkable collection, including rare cards and memorabilia that celebrated the history of various sports. Olbermann's extensive collection gained public attention when he showcased it in various media appearances, sharing his knowledge and enthusiasm with a wider audience. His story exemplifies how collecting can serve as a celebration of history, connecting fans to the athletes and moments that have shaped their lives.

In the realm of pop culture, few collectors have made a mark like Stephen King. The celebrated author, known for his mastery of horror fiction, is also an avid collector of vintage horror memorabilia. King's passion for collecting began in his youth, shaped by his love for the genre that would later define his career. He has amassed a collection that includes rare movie posters, books, and artifacts related to classic horror films. King's enthusiasm for collecting informs not only his writing but also his understanding of the genre's evolution. His story illustrates how personal interests can intersect with professional pursuits, enriching both the collector's life and the cultural landscape.

The tales of these collectors reveal that the act of gathering items transcends mere acquisition. Each story is imbued with purpose, reflecting a desire to connect with history, culture, and personal identity. Collecting becomes a vehicle for storytelling, allowing individuals to share their passions and insights with others. The relationships formed around shared interests can foster community, inspire collaboration, and ignite new ideas.

Moreover, the impact of these collectors often extends beyond their personal journeys. Their dedication to their collections can lead to broader societal changes, influencing trends in art, culture, and preservation. They serve as ambassadors, advocating for their passions and educating others about the significance of the objects they cherish. Whether it's Getty promoting the importance of art, Hummel celebrating folk traditions, or Olbermann connecting fans with sports history, their stories underscore the transformative power of collecting.

In reflecting on the lives of these famous collectors, we see that the reasons behind their pursuits are as diverse as the collections themselves. Some are driven by nostalgia, while others are fueled by a quest for knowledge or a passion for a specific genre. What unites them is a profound love for the stories embedded in the objects they gather. As aspiring collectors, we can draw inspiration from their journeys, recognizing that our own collecting endeavors can lead to meaningful narratives that enrich not only our lives but also the lives of others.

The stories of famous collectors remind us that behind every object lies a deeper significance, a connection to the past, and a bridge to the future. Their legacies inspire us to embrace our passions, share our discoveries, and celebrate the narratives that unite us in the world of collecting. Ultimately, it is through these stories that we find a sense of belonging, purpose, and connection within the vast and diverse community of collectors.

Analyzing the Emotional Value of Collectibles

Collectibles often evoke a powerful emotional response, transcending their material worth to touch the very core of human experience. Each item in a collection carries a weight of sentiment, a story that resonates with the collector's life, memories, and aspirations. This emotional value can be complex, intertwining nostalgia, identity, and connection, making the act of collecting a deeply personal journey.

When we think about nostalgia, it often surfaces as a primary motivator behind many collections. Imagine a middle-aged man who starts gathering vintage baseball cards reminiscent of his childhood. Each card transports him back to sun-soaked afternoons spent playing catch with his father. The crackle of the card's surface and the vibrant images of athletes evoke memories of laughter, camaraderie, and simpler times. For him, these cards are not mere pieces of cardboard; they are vessels of cherished moments, encapsulating a sense of belonging and joy. The emotional value derived from nostalgia can be profound, as it allows collectors to reconnect with their past while celebrating the relationships and experiences that have shaped their lives.

This connection to the past often extends beyond personal memories. Collectors may find themselves drawn to items that represent broader cultural or historical significance. A woman might collect vintage clothing from the 1960s, inspired by the revolutionary spirit of that era. Each garment not only reflects her personal style but also symbolizes a time of social change and empowerment. By curating this collection, she engages with a narrative larger than herself, embracing the struggles and triumphs of those who came before her. The emotional resonance of these items stems from their ability to bridge generations, allowing collectors to feel a part of something greater.

Identity plays a significant role in the emotional landscape of collecting as well. The items we choose to gather often reflect our values, interests, and personalities. A collector of rare books may find solace in the written word, viewing each volume as a gateway to new worlds and ideas. The collection becomes a manifestation of their intellectual pursuits, showcasing their dedication to literature and learning. In this way, collecting serves as a form of self-expression, allowing individuals to curate their identities through the items they cherish. The emotional value lies in the affirmation of self that comes from surrounding oneself with objects that resonate on a personal level.

Furthermore, the act of collecting can foster connections with others, creating a sense of community that enhances the emotional experience. Consider the story of a young woman who begins collecting vinyl records. As she explores thrift shops and record stores, she discovers a vibrant community of fellow enthusiasts. Shared passions lead to friendships formed over discussions about favorite albums and artists. The emotional value derived from these connections cannot be overstated; collecting becomes a shared language that transcends age, background, and geography. The joy of discovering a rare record is amplified when celebrated with others who understand its significance. Together, they create a tapestry of shared experiences, reinforcing the idea that collecting is not just an individual pursuit but also a communal celebration.

The emotional attachment to collectibles can also be influenced by the stories behind the items themselves. A collector of antiques may be drawn to a specific piece not just for its aesthetic beauty but for the history it represents. Imagine finding a delicate porcelain vase that once belonged to a prominent family from centuries past. The thought of its journey through time, the hands it has passed through, and the stories it could tell spark the collector's imagination. This narrative adds layers of meaning, transforming the vase into a cherished artifact that embodies the passage of time and the continuity of human experience. The emotional value is derived from the connection to history, allowing collectors to feel as if they are custodians of the past.

While the emotional value of collectibles is often positive, it can also be tinged with complexities. Collecting can become a coping mechanism for some, a way to fill voids or escape from reality. An individual might find themselves drawn to acquiring items during periods of stress or loneliness. In these instances, the emotional connection can be complicated, leading to a cycle of acquisition that may not necessarily fulfill the deeper emotional needs. The challenge lies in recognizing when collecting serves as a healthy outlet for expression versus when it becomes an unhealthy obsession. This awareness is crucial, as it enables collectors to maintain a balanced relationship with their pursuits, ensuring that their collecting journeys remain fulfilling rather than burdensome.

Moreover, the emotional value of collectibles can be influenced by external factors such as market trends and societal perceptions. Items once considered worthless may suddenly gain popularity, driving collectors to reassess the significance of their belongings. The emotional landscape shifts as items become symbols of status or investment, potentially overshadowing the personal connections that originally inspired the collection. This phenomenon can lead to tensions within collecting communities, as the motivations behind gathering items become more commercialized. For many, the challenge lies in navigating this complex terrain, striving to honor the emotional roots of their collections while engaging with the evolving marketplace.

Ultimately, the emotional value of collectibles is a multifaceted tapestry woven from threads of memory, identity, connection, and narrative. Each item tells a story, inviting the collector to reflect on their journey and the significance of the things they gather. Collecting, at its core, becomes an exploration of the self, a way to navigate the complexities of life through the tangible and the meaningful. Whether spurred by nostalgia, a quest for identity, or the joy of community, the emotional dimensions of collecting enrich our lives in profound ways.

As collectors continue to curate their collections, they engage in a dialogue with their past, present, and future. Each item serves as a reminder of the journey undertaken, the lessons learned, and the connections forged. The emotional value inherent in collecting transforms it from a simple hobby into a profound exploration of what it means to be human. Every collection is a testament to the stories we tell, the memories we cherish, and the bonds we create, illustrating the enduring power of the objects we hold dear.

Inspiring Stories of Unexpected Finds

The thrill of discovery can transform an ordinary day into an extraordinary adventure, especially for collectors who often stumble upon unexpected treasures. These serendipitous finds not only enrich collections but also forge unforgettable memories and connections. Each story of an unexpected discovery reveals the magic of chance and the joy that can come from exploring the world with open eyes and an adventurous spirit.

Consider the tale of a young man named Alex, who had always been fascinated by vintage bicycles. One summer afternoon, he decided to visit a local flea market, not necessarily in search of anything specific but hoping to soak in the atmosphere and perhaps find a unique piece to add to his modest collection. As he wandered through the maze of stalls, filled with trinkets and antiques, something caught his eye—a rusty, old bicycle leaning against a weathered table. At first glance, it seemed like just another forgotten relic, but as he approached, he noticed details that hinted at its history. The intricate engravings on the frame and the faded logo of a long-defunct manufacturer piqued his curiosity.

With a sense of excitement bubbling inside him, Alex began to negotiate with the vendor, who seemed unaware of the bicycle's true potential. After some back-and-forth, he managed to purchase the bike at a fraction of its worth. When he got it home, Alex meticulously cleaned and restored the bicycle, uncovering layers of beauty hidden beneath years of neglect. The vintage bike turned out to be a rare model from the late 1940s, a piece that not only enhanced his collection but also sparked connections with fellow enthusiasts who appreciated its historical significance. This unexpected find became a centerpiece of his collection and a story he would share for years to come, illustrating how a simple visit to a flea market can lead to remarkable discoveries.

Another inspiring story comes from a woman named Clara, who had long been captivated by the world of antiques. One rainy afternoon, she decided to visit an estate sale in her neighborhood, hoping to find a few decorative items for her home. As she sifted through boxes filled with trinkets, she stumbled upon a dusty, leather-bound book tucked away in a corner. Intrigued, she opened it to discover it was a journal belonging to a soldier from World War II. The pages were filled with handwritten notes, sketches, and photographs that captured the soldier's experiences during the war.

Clara felt an immediate connection to the journal, as if she had been granted access to a personal narrative that conveyed both the struggles and triumphs of a life lived in extraordinary times. She decided to purchase the journal, and that decision led her down a path of research and discovery. With each page, she learned more about the soldier's life, the historical context of his experiences, and the impact of the war on families and communities. The journal became a catalyst for Clara to share the soldier's story with others, igniting her passion for history and storytelling. What began as a casual visit to an estate sale transformed into a profound exploration of the past, blending her love for antiques with a newfound commitment to preserving history through storytelling.

The thrill of the unexpected also resonates in the story of Ben, a collector of comic books and memorabilia. He often frequented comic book shops, but one day, he decided to stop by a garage sale in his neighborhood. Among the various household items, he spotted a cardboard box overflowing with comic books, their covers frayed and pages yellowed with age. As he began to sift through the stack, he felt a rush of adrenaline. Hidden within the pile was a first edition of a legendary comic book series, one that had been out of print for decades and was highly sought after by collectors.

Ben knew he had struck gold. He negotiated a price with the seller, who had no idea of the treasure they had in their midst. The thrill of the find reinvigorated

Ben's passion for collecting. He carefully preserved the comic book, and it quickly became a highlight of his collection. It also led him to connect with other collectors who shared his enthusiasm, opening doors to new friendships and opportunities to discuss their shared interests. Ben's unexpected find not only enhanced his collection but also deepened his love for the community of collectors he had come to cherish.

Stories of unexpected finds often transcend the individual, illustrating the power of community and shared experiences. A group of friends who regularly visited thrift stores together stumbled upon an old, dusty painting in the corner of a shop. Initially, it seemed unremarkable, but upon closer inspection, they noticed a signature in the corner that looked familiar. After some research, they discovered that the painting was created by a local artist whose works had been lost to time. The friends decided to purchase the painting and organized a small exhibition to showcase their find.

Through their efforts, they not only celebrated the artist's legacy but also engaged the community in a discussion about the importance of preserving local art and history. This unexpected find became a catalyst for dialogue, bringing people together and fostering a greater appreciation for the art within their own community. The joy of discovery transformed into a collective celebration, illustrating how a simple thrift store visit can lead to meaningful connections and shared experiences.

The emotional resonance of unexpected finds is undeniable. Each story reflects the excitement of discovery and the potential for transformation that lies within seemingly mundane moments. Whether it's a vintage bicycle, a soldier's journal, a valuable comic book, or a hidden painting, the thrill of uncovering these treasures reminds us of the richness of life and the stories that surround us.

The art of collecting, then, is not merely about acquiring items; it is about the experiences, connections, and narratives woven into each find. Every unexpected discovery adds a layer of meaning to the collector's journey, serving as a reminder that the world is full of hidden gems waiting to be uncovered. The thrill of the hunt, combined with the joy of sharing these stories, transforms collecting into an adventure, one that connects us to our past, enriches our present, and inspires our future. By embracing the possibility of unexpected finds, we open ourselves up to a world of wonder, where every corner holds the potential for discovery and every item tells a story waiting to be told.

The Legacy of Collections

Collections often serve as more than just a compilation of items; they embody legacies that reflect personal histories, cultural narratives, and social movements. The act of collecting transcends mere accumulation; it is a profound expression of identity, passion, and continuity. Each collection tells a story, weaving together the past and present while leaving a mark on the future. As we delve into the legacy of collections, we uncover how they shape our understanding of the world and our place within it.

Consider the story of a man named David, whose fascination with vintage toys began in his childhood. Growing up in a modest neighborhood, he found joy in collecting action figures and model cars, often using them as props in elaborate adventures played out in his backyard. As David aged, the toys became symbols of his youthful imagination and creativity. They represented a time when life was filled with wonder and possibility. Over the years, his collection expanded to include toys from different eras, each piece serving as a portal to a specific moment in time.

David's collection gradually evolved into a curated display that reflected not only his personal journey but also the evolution of toy design and cultural trends. Friends and family marveled at the collection, and what began as a solitary hobby blossomed into a communal experience. David started hosting open houses, inviting fellow collectors and curious neighbors to explore the world of vintage toys. The gatherings became opportunities for storytelling, as attendees shared their own childhood memories and experiences with toys, reinforcing the idea that these objects carry emotional weight and shared cultural significance.

Through David's collection, connections were forged, and friendships blossomed. It became clear that his toys were not merely relics of the past; they were vessels of nostalgia, bridging generational gaps and fostering intergenerational dialogue. The legacy of his collection extended beyond the items themselves, creating a space for community and shared memories. The stories exchanged during these gatherings enriched the experience, highlighting how collecting can serve as a means of preserving and celebrating cultural heritage.

Art collections also illustrate the profound legacy that can emerge from the act of gathering. Take, for instance, the story of a woman named Sarah, who was captivated by contemporary art. After inheriting a modest sum from her grandmother, she decided to invest in pieces that resonated with her personal aesthetic. What started as a small endeavor quickly transformed into a passionate pursuit, as Sarah sought out emerging artists and established her own collection.

Over time, Sarah's collection grew into a diverse array of artworks that captured the zeitgeist of her generation. Each piece resonated with her experiences, reflecting societal issues, personal struggles, and triumphs. As Sarah began to understand the artists' backgrounds and the stories behind their work, her collection evolved into a platform for advocacy and awareness. She organized exhibitions that showcased not only her collection but also the narratives that accompanied each piece, sparking conversations about the role of art in society and its ability to inspire change.

Through her dedication to the arts, Sarah became a champion for underrepresented voices in the art community. She used her collection to support local artists and foster a sense of belonging within the creative landscape. The legacy of her collection extended beyond her personal enjoyment; it became a catalyst for social dialogue and empowerment, illustrating how collections can shape cultural conversations and influence future generations.

The legacy of collections can also be seen in the realm of historical artifacts. Institutions like museums and libraries serve as guardians of our collective memory, preserving items that tell the stories of our past. A small town museum may house artifacts from its founding days, including tools, photographs, and documents that offer insights into the lives of early settlers. These collections become invaluable resources for historians, researchers, and the community at large, providing tangible connections to history.

For example, a local history museum might display a collection of letters written by a soldier during World War II. These letters, filled with personal reflections and experiences, not only offer a glimpse into the soldier's life but also illuminate the broader historical context of the war. Visitors who engage with such collections often leave with a deeper understanding of their community's history and the sacrifices made by those who came before them. The legacy of these collections lies in their ability to educate and inspire, reminding us of the importance of preserving our shared heritage.

Moreover, collections can impact future generations in unexpected ways. Consider a family that has passed down a collection of heirloom quilts, each one representing a significant moment in their history. As each quilt is stitched together, it tells a story—of love, loss, celebration, or resilience. When the quilts are handed down to the next generation, they carry with them not only the craftsmanship of the past but also the stories of those who created them. This legacy fosters a sense of belonging and continuity, connecting family members through shared narratives and traditions.

In this way, collecting becomes an act of stewardship, where individuals take on the responsibility of preserving and sharing the stories that enrich their lives. The quilts serve as reminders of family bonds, cultural heritage, and the importance of storytelling in shaping identity. Each time a new generation engages with the collection, it reinforces the legacy, ensuring that the stories continue to be told and cherished.

The impact of collections extends far beyond the individual; it resonates within communities, cultures, and societies. They serve as repositories of memory, offering insights into the human experience across time and space. Whether through toys, art, historical artifacts, or family heirlooms, the legacy of collections reminds us of the interconnectedness of our stories. They invite us to reflect on our past, celebrate our present, and inspire our future.

As we navigate the world of collecting, it becomes evident that these endeavors are not solely about acquiring possessions. They are about cultivating connections, preserving legacies, and fostering understanding. The emotional and cultural significance embedded within collections enriches our lives, providing a lens through which we can explore the complexities of human experience. Ultimately, the legacy of collections lies in their ability to transcend

time, connecting us to our roots while guiding us
toward the future we wish to create.

Chapter 7: The Future of Small Collections

Trends in Collecting

The landscape of collecting is constantly evolving, shaped by cultural shifts, technological advancements, and societal changes. What was once a niche hobby for a select group has transformed into a vibrant global phenomenon, attracting enthusiasts from all walks of life. As people seek to express their identities and connect with others, trends in collecting emerge, reflecting broader themes and interests that resonate within society.

One of the most significant trends in recent years is the rise of digital collectibles, particularly in the form of non-fungible tokens (NFTs). These unique digital assets have captivated collectors and investors alike, allowing individuals to own and trade one-of-a-kind pieces of art, music, and even virtual real estate. The appeal of NFTs lies in their ability to provide provenance and authenticity in the digital realm, a crucial aspect for collectors who value originality. Artists find new avenues for expression and monetization, while collectors relish the opportunity to own a piece of digital history. This trend has democratized the art world, enabling emerging artists to gain recognition and connect with collectors globally. The buzz around NFTs represents a broader cultural shift toward valuing digital experiences, making it a defining characteristic of contemporary collecting.

Alongside the digital revolution, vintage and retro items have surged in popularity. Nostalgia plays a powerful role in this trend, as individuals seek comfort in the familiar artifacts of their past. Collectors are increasingly drawn to items from the 1980s and 1990s, from toys and video games to fashion and pop culture memorabilia. The resurgence of platforms like eBay and Etsy has made it easier than ever to find these treasures, leading to a flourishing market for vintage goods. Thrift stores and flea markets are bustling with activity, as treasure hunters scour the aisles for hidden gems. This trend speaks to a collective yearning for connection to simpler times and cherished memories, reflecting a desire to reclaim the joy of youth.

Sustainability and ethical considerations have also become central to the collecting ethos. As awareness of environmental issues grows, many collectors are shifting their focus toward sustainable practices. This includes seeking out eco-friendly materials, supporting local artisans, and collecting items with a story—a narrative that often involves recycling or upcycling. Vintage clothing, for example, has gained immense traction as individuals recognize the impact of fast fashion on the planet. Collectors are not only curating personal wardrobes but also investing in a sustainable future. This trend encourages a mindfulness that extends beyond personal enjoyment, intertwining the act of collecting with a commitment to social responsibility.

Moreover, the world of collecting has become increasingly inclusive. Historically, certain types of collections were dominated by specific demographics, but today, diverse voices and narratives are being celebrated. This shift is evident in the rise of marginalized artists and creators who are gaining recognition within the collecting community. Collectors are increasingly interested in works that challenge conventional norms and reflect a variety of perspectives. Gender, race, and cultural identity are now significant considerations in the art and collectibles market, leading to a more dynamic and representative landscape. This trend not only enriches the collecting experience but also fosters a sense of belonging and shared understanding among collectors.

The influence of social media cannot be overstated in the realm of collecting. Platforms like Instagram and TikTok have transformed how collectors connect, share, and showcase their treasures. Collecting has become a visual medium, with curated feeds serving as galleries for individuals to display their collections and engage with like-minded enthusiasts. Hashtags and challenges create a sense of community, allowing collectors to bond over shared passions and discover new interests. This digital camaraderie has led to the emergence of micro-communities centered around specific types of collectibles, from action figures to rare stamps. The accessibility of social media has not only broadened the audience for collecting but has also empowered individuals to share their stories and experiences, enriching the overall culture of collecting.

As we embrace the future, technology continues to play a pivotal role in shaping trends in collecting. Virtual reality (VR) and augmented reality (AR) are beginning to redefine how we experience collections. Imagine walking through a virtual museum, exploring exhibits that feature interactive displays and immersive environments. With VR, collectors can engage with their items in ways that were previously unimaginable, fostering a deeper appreciation for the stories behind each piece. Similarly, AR allows users to visualize how items might fit within their own collections or living spaces, making the collecting experience more dynamic and personalized.

Additionally, the rise of subscription boxes has transformed how collectors acquire items. These curated packages deliver surprise collectibles to subscribers on a regular basis, catering to specific interests—from comic books to artisanal crafts. This trend not only adds an element of excitement to the collecting process but also fosters a sense of discovery as collectors eagerly await their next shipment. The convenience and thrill of subscription services have made them an attractive option for both seasoned collectors and newcomers alike, further expanding the reach of collecting as a hobby.

As trends in collecting continue to evolve, they reflect the changing fabric of society and the diverse interests of individuals. The digital age has opened doors to new possibilities, while nostalgia, sustainability, inclusivity, and technological advancements shape the collecting landscape. Each trend offers a glimpse into the values and aspirations of collectors, highlighting their desire to connect, express themselves, and preserve cultural narratives.

In this dynamic environment, the act of collecting remains a deeply personal and meaningful pursuit. It invites individuals to explore their passions, connect with others, and engage with the world around them. As every trend unfolds, collectors will undoubtedly adapt and innovate, ensuring that the spirit of collecting remains vibrant and relevant for generations to come. Each unique collection is not merely a reflection of its owner but a testament to the rich tapestry of human experience, woven together through shared stories, memories, and aspirations. The legacy of collecting continues to thrive, capturing the essence of who we are and how we relate to the world.

The Impact of Technology on Collecting

The evolution of technology has fundamentally reshaped the landscape of collecting, transforming how enthusiasts engage with their passions and interact with the objects they cherish. From the advent of the internet to the rise of digital platforms, technology has ushered in unprecedented changes, making the act of collecting more accessible, dynamic, and interconnected than ever before. The impact of these advancements extends beyond mere convenience; it alters the very essence of what it means to be a collector.

Consider the way collectors once relied on physical catalogs or local shops to discover new items. The process was often laborious, requiring extensive travel and time spent flipping through pages or rummaging through shelves. Today, the internet serves as a vast marketplace, teeming with opportunities for discovery. Websites dedicated to collectibles provide an expansive array of items from around the globe, allowing enthusiasts to explore categories that pique their interest. Whether it's vintage vinyl records, rare comic books, or antique furniture, collectors can now browse, compare, and purchase with a few clicks. This accessibility has democratized collecting, breaking down geographical barriers and enabling individuals to curate collections that reflect their unique tastes.

Moreover, social media platforms have revolutionized how collectors share their passions. Instagram, Facebook, and dedicated forums have become vibrant hubs where enthusiasts showcase their collections, connect with others, and exchange knowledge. A collector in one part of the world can instantly share images of their latest acquisition with a community that spans continents. This interconnectedness fosters a sense of belonging and camaraderie, as individuals bond over shared interests and experiences. Hashtags and online challenges further enhance engagement, encouraging collectors to participate in conversations and showcase their items in creative ways. The thrill of discovery is no longer limited to the physical realm; it thrives in the digital space, where ideas and inspiration flow freely.

The rise of mobile applications has also transformed the collecting experience. Apps designed for collectors provide tools for inventory management, price tracking, and community engagement. Imagine having a comprehensive database of your collection at your fingertips, complete with photographs, purchase history, and estimated values. These apps not only enhance organization but also empower collectors to make informed decisions when buying or selling items. Such technological advancements streamline the collecting process, allowing enthusiasts to focus on what truly matters: their passion for collecting.

Digital technology has also introduced new forms of collectibles that challenge traditional notions. The emergence of non-fungible tokens (NFTs) has created a seismic shift in how we perceive ownership and value in the digital age. Artists and creators can now produce unique digital assets that exist on the blockchain, granting collectors the ability to own one-of-a-kind pieces of art, music, or virtual experiences. This innovation has attracted a new generation of collectors who view digital art as a legitimate medium, blurring the lines between traditional and contemporary forms of collecting. The allure of NFTs lies in their scarcity and the provenance they offer, allowing collectors to invest in digital culture in ways previously unimaginable.

As technology continues to evolve, augmented reality (AR) and virtual reality (VR) are poised to revolutionize how collectors interact with their items. Imagine stepping into a virtual space that showcases your collection, allowing you to explore and appreciate your items in a lifelike environment. AR can enhance the physical collecting experience by providing additional context, such as historical information or interactive features when viewing an item through a smartphone. These technologies create immersive experiences that deepen the emotional connection between collectors and their objects, transforming how we engage with the stories behind each piece.

The impact of technology extends beyond individual collectors; it influences the broader market as well. Online auction platforms have gained immense popularity, enabling collectors to bid on items from the comfort of their homes. This shift has transformed the auction house experience, allowing more participants to engage in bidding wars for coveted items. The transparency provided by online platforms means that collectors can easily research prices and trends, leveling the playing field and ensuring that informed decisions are made. This accessibility has led to more diverse participation in the collecting community, fostering a dynamic marketplace that thrives on competition and innovation.

However, the integration of technology into collecting is not without its challenges. The ease of access to online marketplaces can sometimes lead to issues of authenticity and quality. Unscrupulous sellers may take advantage of unsuspecting buyers, offering counterfeit or misrepresented items. As a result, collectors must remain vigilant and educated about their areas of interest. The onus is on individuals to conduct thorough research and seek reputable sources, ensuring that their collections are built on a foundation of trust and integrity.

Additionally, the rapid pace of technological change can create a sense of overwhelm. With new platforms and trends emerging regularly, collectors may find it challenging to keep up. Balancing the excitement of innovation with the desire for meaningful connections to their collections can be a delicate dance. Collectors must navigate this landscape thoughtfully, recognizing that technology is a tool to enhance their experience rather than a replacement for the emotional ties that bind them to their objects.

Sustainability in Collecting

The conversation surrounding sustainability has permeated every aspect of modern life, and collecting is no exception. As awareness of environmental issues grows, collectors are increasingly reevaluating their practices, seeking ways to engage with their passions while minimizing their ecological footprint. This shift toward sustainability reflects a broader societal movement that values ethical consumption and the preservation of resources for future generations.

Sustainability in collecting manifests in various forms, from the types of items individuals choose to pursue to the methods of acquisition and care for those items. One significant trend is the growing interest in vintage and secondhand items. Instead of purchasing new products that contribute to overconsumption and waste, collectors are turning to thrift stores, flea markets, and online marketplaces to find pre-loved treasures. This not only provides a more unique and personal touch to their collections but also promotes the recycling of goods, reducing the demand for new production and the accompanying environmental impact.

For many collectors, the stories behind vintage items add an extra layer of value. Each piece carries a history, a narrative that connects the past to the present. When you pick up a vintage dress from the 1970s or a classic vinyl record, you're not just acquiring an object; you're inheriting its journey. This appreciation for history often leads to a deeper respect for the materials and craftsmanship involved in creating these items. Collectors become custodians of culture, ensuring that these artifacts are preserved and appreciated for generations to come.

Another important aspect of sustainability is the choice of materials. Many collectors are increasingly drawn to items made from sustainable or recycled materials. For instance, the craft of upcycling—where old or discarded materials are transformed into new products—has gained significant traction. Artists and creators are producing stunning pieces that not only reflect creativity but also embody a commitment to reducing waste. Collectors who seek out these items contribute to a circular economy, where goods are reused and repurposed rather than discarded.

The digital realm has also opened up new avenues for sustainable collecting. The rise of non-fungible tokens (NFTs) and digital art allows collectors to own unique pieces without the physical materials that traditional collecting often entails. While the environmental impact of blockchain technology is a topic of debate, the ability to engage with art and collectibles in a digital format can lessen the pressure on physical resources. It offers an innovative way to appreciate creativity while exploring sustainability.

Moreover, the act of collecting can be a powerful tool for advocacy and awareness. Collectors often use their platforms to highlight issues related to sustainability and environmental protection. For example, an art collector may focus on works that address climate change or promote conservation efforts. This not only raises awareness within the collector community but also encourages others to think critically about their own purchasing habits and the impact of their collections. Through shared narratives and collective action, the potential for change grows exponentially.

The importance of community cannot be overlooked when discussing sustainability in collecting. Many collectors are joining forces to create local networks that emphasize ethical practices. These groups often focus on sharing resources, hosting workshops on sustainable practices, and promoting events that celebrate eco-friendly artisans. By fostering connections, collectors can inspire one another to make environmentally conscious choices, whether it's through sourcing local items, supporting sustainable brands, or engaging in community recycling initiatives.

Caring for collections sustainably is another crucial consideration. Collectors often invest time and resources into preserving their items, and there are eco-friendly methods to consider. For example, using natural cleaning products, sustainable storage solutions, and materials that don't contribute to pollution can enhance the longevity of a collection while minimizing its environmental impact. By adopting sustainable care practices, collectors ensure their items remain in excellent condition without compromising their ecological values.

Despite the positive strides being made, challenges remain. The world of collecting can sometimes foster a culture of excess, where the thrill of acquiring new items overshadows concerns for sustainability. This is particularly evident in certain subcultures, where the drive for the latest release or rare find can lead to impulsive purchases. To combat this, collectors are encouraged to cultivate a mindful approach, focusing on quality over quantity. By thoughtfully considering each acquisition and its implications, collectors can create meaningful collections that reflect their values.

Another challenge lies in the transition to sustainable practices. Many collectors may feel overwhelmed by the multitude of options available, unsure of where to begin. Education and awareness are vital in this regard. Providing resources, sharing success stories, and highlighting sustainable practices can empower individuals to make informed choices. Whether through blogs, social media, or workshops, fostering a culture of knowledge can ignite a passion for sustainability within the collecting community.

As the landscape of collecting continues to evolve, the integration of sustainability will shape the future of the hobby. Collectors who embrace eco-friendly practices not only enhance their own experiences but also contribute to a broader movement towards responsible consumption. The act of collecting becomes a celebration of creativity, history, and ethics, transforming it into something far more significant than mere acquisition.

Ultimately, sustainability in collecting is about balance. It is the intersection of passion and responsibility, where the joy of acquiring unique items coexists with a commitment to preserving the planet. Collectors have the power to influence trends and norms, paving the way for a more sustainable future. As they curate their collections, they also curate a legacy—one that honors the past while nurturing the world for future generations. Each choice made in this journey resonates far beyond individual collections, contributing to a collective effort that values the planet and its resources. Through thoughtful collecting, we can all play a part in crafting a more sustainable narrative, one item at a time.

Preserving Small Histories for Future Generations

Every object tells a story. Often, these stories are woven into the very fabric of our lives, capturing moments, emotions, and experiences that define who we are. Preserving small histories is an act of love and remembrance, a way to honor the past while ensuring that future generations can connect with the lives and experiences that shaped their world. In an age where the rapid pace of change can sometimes feel overwhelming, the importance of safeguarding these narratives becomes increasingly paramount.

The concept of small histories encompasses everyday items, family heirlooms, photographs, letters, and even oral traditions passed down through generations. Each of these elements contributes to a rich tapestry of personal and collective memory. Consider a simple wooden toy that once belonged to a grandparent. It may appear unremarkable at first glance, but it is imbued with the laughter of childhood, the creativity of play, and the love of a family. By preserving such items, we encapsulate the essence of those moments, allowing future generations to glimpse the joys and challenges of their ancestors.

One powerful method of preservation is through storytelling. Sharing stories about the items we cherish helps to root them in context. When you tell your child about the significance of a vintage brooch worn by their great-grandmother at special occasions, you transfer not just a piece of jewelry but a legacy of love and tradition. These narratives breathe life into objects, turning them from mere possessions into vessels of memory. They become windows through which future generations can view their heritage, fostering a sense of identity and belonging.

Photography plays a crucial role in preserving small histories. As technology has advanced, we now have the ability to capture moments instantaneously. However, the essence of photography goes beyond the act of clicking a button; it is about what those images represent. A photograph of a family gathering or a candid moment at a picnic freezes time, encapsulating emotions that can be revisited and shared. It is vital to not only take these photographs but also to organize and annotate them. Writing down the names of people, places, and events connected to each image ensures that the stories behind the pictures remain alive. In doing so, we create a visual archive that transcends generations.

In addition to personal objects and photographs, preserving the written word is equally significant.

Letters, diaries, and journals provide intimate insights into the lives of those who came before us. They capture thoughts, dreams, and challenges in a way that transcends time. Imagine discovering a letter written by a great-uncle during a historical event, detailing his experiences and emotions. Such documents offer a unique perspective, allowing us to understand the past through the eyes of those who lived it. Archiving these materials, whether through digital preservation or careful physical storage, ensures that they survive the test of time.

Oral histories represent another vital aspect of preserving small histories. The practice of sharing stories verbally has existed for millennia and remains a powerful way to connect with the past. Engaging older family members in conversations about their lives can yield a treasure trove of information. Recording these conversations, whether through audio or video, captures not just the content but also the emotion and inflection of the storyteller's voice. These recordings become invaluable resources for future generations, offering them a chance to hear the wisdom and experiences of their ancestors firsthand.

As we pursue the preservation of small histories, technology offers innovative solutions. Digital archives, social media, and online platforms allow us to share and safeguard our collections in ways that were previously unimaginable. Creating a family website or a social media group dedicated to sharing memories can foster community and encourage participation from family members near and far. This digital footprint can serve as a modern-day scrapbook, where stories, images, and heirlooms can be easily accessed and cherished.

However, the preservation of small histories is not without its challenges. The fast-paced nature of contemporary life often leads to the neglect of personal artifacts. Items can be discarded or forgotten, and stories can fade into obscurity if not actively maintained. To combat this, it is essential to cultivate a mindset focused on preservation. Encouraging family members to engage with and respect their heritage fosters a culture of remembrance. Regular family gatherings can provide opportunities to share stories and revisit cherished items, creating a ritual around preservation.

Another challenge lies in the fleeting nature of digital storage. While technology offers convenience, it is important to remember that digital formats can become obsolete. Regularly backing up important files and ensuring that family histories are stored in multiple formats—both physical and digital—can mitigate the risk of loss. This proactive approach reinforces the idea that preserving small histories is an ongoing commitment.

In a world that often prioritizes the grand and the spectacular, the importance of small histories can be overlooked. Yet, it is precisely these small stories that anchor us, grounding us in a shared human experience. The act of preserving them is an affirmation of our identities, a way to acknowledge where we came from and how we are connected to one another. They remind us that every life, no matter how ordinary it may seem, contributes to the larger narrative of humanity.

As we reflect on the importance of preserving small histories, we must recognize our role as custodians of memory. It is our responsibility to honor the stories of those who came before us, ensuring that their legacies endure. By valuing and safeguarding these narratives, we create a bridge between generations, enriching the lives of both the present and the future. Through storytelling, photography, written records, and oral traditions, we weave a rich tapestry of connections that celebrate our shared heritage. In this way, we ensure that the small histories that define us are not lost to time but are cherished and passed down, illuminating the past for those yet to come.

Embracing Change in the Collecting World

Change is the only constant in life, a truth that resonates deeply within the world of collecting. As enthusiasts navigate the evolving landscape of their passions, they must learn to embrace transformation, adapting to new trends, technologies, and cultural shifts. This journey is not merely about the act of acquiring items; it is a reflection of the dynamic relationship between collectors and the world around them. The ability to adapt to change can enhance the collecting experience, providing opportunities for growth, connection, and discovery.

The rise of digital technology has revolutionized how collectors engage with their interests. Once reliant on brick-and-mortar stores, collectors now have access to online marketplaces that offer a vast array of items from all over the globe. Websites dedicated to collectibles, auction platforms, and social media groups have created a vibrant ecosystem where enthusiasts can connect, share, and trade. This shift has broadened the scope of collecting, allowing individuals to discover niche items that may not have been available in their local communities. Embracing these platforms means embracing a new way of sourcing and sharing, fostering a sense of community that transcends geographic boundaries.

Social media has transformed the way collectors showcase their collections and connect with others. Instagram, for instance, has become a visual diary for collectors, where they can share images of their prized possessions and interact with like-minded individuals. Hashtags allow for the discovery of new trends and communities, expanding the reach of individual collectors. This shift has not only democratized the world of collecting but also encouraged creativity and expression. Collectors now curate their online presence, using storytelling techniques to weave narratives around their collections, elevating their significance beyond mere items.

As new generations of collectors emerge, their perspectives on collecting are reshaping the landscape. Young collectors often prioritize sustainability and ethical sourcing, challenging traditional notions of what it means to collect. They seek out vintage and secondhand items, valuing the stories attached to them and the environmental benefits of reusing materials. This shift in mindset encourages seasoned collectors to reconsider their own practices, fostering a dialogue about the importance of conscious collecting. Embracing these new values can enrich collections and create a legacy that resonates with future generations.

The impact of technology extends beyond sourcing and sharing; it also transforms how collectors document and preserve their collections. Digital tools enable enthusiasts to maintain detailed inventories, track the history and value of their items, and even create virtual exhibitions. These advancements empower collectors to organize their passions systematically, making it easier to reflect on their journey. As technology continues to evolve, collectors can leverage new innovations for archiving and sharing their collections, ensuring that their stories endure.

Yet, with change comes uncertainty. The rapid pace of technological development can be daunting, particularly for those who have built their collections through traditional means. The fear of obsolescence looms large, as collectors wonder whether their beloved practices will be rendered outdated. It is essential, however, to view change as an opportunity rather than a threat. By embracing new tools and methodologies, collectors can enhance their experiences and create richer, more meaningful connections with their items and the community.

The collecting world is also influenced by shifting cultural trends. What was once considered a niche interest may suddenly become mainstream, altering the value and perception of specific items. For example, the renewed interest in retro video games, fueled by nostalgia and the rise of gaming culture, has led to a surge in demand for consoles and cartridges that were once deemed obsolete. This phenomenon demonstrates how societal changes can breathe new life into collecting, encouraging enthusiasts to explore new avenues and expand their horizons.

Adapting to these cultural shifts requires an open mind. Collectors must be willing to explore items beyond their established preferences, discovering new genres, styles, and eras. This willingness to embrace change can lead to unexpected joys and connections, as collectors stumble upon items that resonate with them in profound ways. Engaging with diverse collecting communities can also provide fresh perspectives, enriching one's understanding of the broader context in which their collections exist.

Moreover, embracing change can enhance the narrative of a collection. Each new addition tells a story, contributing to the overall tapestry of experiences that define a collector's journey. By welcoming new influences, collectors can create a narrative that reflects their evolution, capturing the essence of their passions over time. This ongoing story becomes a living testament to their interests, encouraging reflection and growth.

Collaboration within the collecting community can further amplify the benefits of embracing change. Collectors who share their knowledge, experiences, and resources can foster an environment of learning and creativity. Workshops, exhibitions, and online forums provide platforms for discussion and exploration, enabling individuals to learn from one another and adapt to new ideas. This spirit of collaboration nurtures a sense of belonging, reinforcing the notion that collecting is not just an individual pursuit but a collective experience.

As the world of collecting continues to evolve, the ability to adapt becomes increasingly vital. Enthusiasts who embrace change open themselves to a wealth of opportunities, from discovering new items to forming lasting connections. The journey of collecting is not merely about amassing possessions but about engaging with the stories, cultures, and innovations that shape our world. By remaining open to transformation, collectors can cultivate a deeper appreciation for their passions, ensuring that their collections remain vibrant and relevant in an ever-changing landscape.

www.ingramcontent.com/pod-product-compliance
Lightning Source LLC
Chambersburg PA
CBHW061305120726

48001CB00001B/480